GROWING UP IN FULHAM

GROWING UP IN FULHAM

Memories of SW6
1940–1953

HARRY TURNER

ISIS
LARGE PRINT
Oxford

First published in Great Britain 2004
by
Janus Publishing Company Ltd

Published in Large Print 2005 by ISIS Publishing Ltd,
7 C_____ad, Osney Mead, Oxford OX2 0ES
by arrangement with
s Publishing Company Ltd

The moral right of the author has been asserted

British Library Cataloguing in Publication Data
Turner, Harry
    Growing up in Fulham. – Large print ed.
    (Isis reminiscence series)
    1. Turner, Harry – Childhood and youth
    2. Large type books
    3. London (England) – Social life and customs
    4. Fulham (London, England) – Biography
    I. Title
    942.1'33085'092

ISBN 0–7531–9332–9 (hb)
ISBN 0–7531–9333–7 (pb)

Printed and bound in Great Britain by
T. J. International Ltd., Padstow, Cornwall

For Gregory and Jane

CONTENTS

A Lament For The 1950s

It was said of the 1960s that, it was less of a decade and more of a swinging epoch. It was both innocent and sinful, wise and foolish, and it burnt with a fierce bright flame for the whole of its gaudy ten years.

It was an age of mushrooming affluence and surly adolescence and of glass ceilings being shattered, of designer cockney accents and a new assertiveness among the young.

The late 1940s, by comparison, were austere, bruised, glad-to-have-survived, watching your Ps and Qs and knowing your place, because people were still licking their wounds, picking their way through the rubble.

The end of the 1940s and early 1950s were only marginally better, but there were still stirrings, the distant drumbeat of challenge, the slightly muffled questioning of authority, little explosions of sartorial subversiveness, draped jackets, gabardine slacks from Cecil Gees, the DA haircut, jazz at Humphrey Littleton's Jazz Club, French kissing.

French kissing?

Absolutely. The first tongue sandwich, it is seriously claimed by aficionados, was given and received in Fulham in 1950 at the Regal Cinema, Walham Green,

1

during a performance by Petula Clark in the brief interval between the "B" feature and the main movie, which was *Gone with the Wind*.

The kiss, not the performance by Petula, was a rite of passage for a fifteen year old whose experience of things carnal up to that moment could best be described as bleak.

But I am getting ahead of myself. This book is not just about the 1950s; it is about life in a particular borough of London during that decade.

I was born in Fulham in 1935 in a street next to Fulham Library and I lived in the Borough until 1953 when I joined the army to do my National Service.

Today, Fulham is a smart, bustling, cosmopolitan London enclave with opulent restaurants, boutiques and glossy, highrise apartments for the upwardly mobile middle class. Its borders seem to have melted into the neighbouring districts of Chelsea and South Kensington and its property prices are rapidly catching up with those of London's most fashionable areas.

BMWs and bulky four wheel drives cram the streets. Old terraces that used to house the urban working class have been gentrified; potted bay trees, fake coaching lamps and lion's head knockers now proliferate.

Famous people reside in Fulham today and you are just as likely to encounter TV celebrities or rising thespians in the North End Road Market as you are to spot them in the King's Road, Chelsea.

The pace of life is different too. Faster, of course, with the Fulham Road, the Borough's main artery to

Putney in the south and Kensington in the north, always jam packed with traffic.

The 14 bus still jogs along the Fulham Road and the 22 still travels the New King's Road past the curiously named World's End.

But now there are art galleries and painfully fashionable little restaurants and flower shops selling dead branches in big glass jars for 60 quid and pubs whose names have been changed to Slug and Lettuce or The Pimple and Sausage?

It wasn't always like this. The earliest mention of Fulham occurs in a Grant of the Manor by Tyrhtilus, Bishop Of Hereford, to the Bishop of London and his successors in AD 691 in which Grant it is called Fulanham. It was formally part of the County of Middlesex and its name derives from the Saxons who originally inhabited it.

Fulham was variously known as Fulanhamme, Foleham and the Fulanham of the 691 ecclesiastical Grant. For reasons lost in the mists of time, the area near the All Saints' Church by the river was, in 1561, called Godeyereshayll.

Below Fulham lies the chalk of the London basin above which is London clay. The first recorded settlement was by the River Thames and others followed: Walham Green, Parson's Green, Sands Ends and North End.

This memoir however, is about more recent times: the period from the end of the Second World War to the early 1950s. These were the years during which I grew up and experienced the first tiny changes in life and

3

social behaviour that have so accelerated in the last decades of the 20th century.

In the early part of my life in Fulham, the Walham Green District had no less than seven pubs: The George, The White Hart, The Swan, The King's Head, The Red Lion, The Maltsters and The Cock, and Walham Green was only a tiny part of Fulham, just a few streets.

There was a profusion of cinemas in the area too. The Walham Green Cinematograph Theatre at 583 Fulham Road, the Broadway Gardens Picture House behind the station, the Fulham Picture Palace, later the Ritz, at 260 North End Road, the Fulham Electric Theatre at number 303 and the wonderfully sleazy Red Hall that later was scrubbed up and became a Gaumont.

We had our own theatre too, the Granville, built in 1900 and founded by the music hall star, Dan Leno. It was something of an architectural wonder, for Fulham at least, having been designed by the flamboyant and prolific theatre architect, Frank Matcham. Sadly it succumbed to the builders' iron ball in 1971.

Being close to the river, Fulham in its early days was susceptible to flooding. Northwards of the Lillie Road, streets were laid on swampy ground called marshcroft and at every high tide, the footpaths were inches under water.

Beaufort House, built there in the late 1800s, became a large lunatic asylum and later the headquarters of the South Middlesex Rifle Volunteers. Over a century and a half later, I was commissioned

4

into the 1st Battalion of the Middlesex Regiment. The H.Q. was demolished in 1904 and the site is now occupied by a large school.

Craven Cottage, now the home of Fulham Football Club, was once a pretty thatched house of Alice-in-Wonderland cuteness and an earlier owner, Lord George Bulwey Lytton, entertained Napoleon III there to cakes and tea. Napoleon is said to have called it, "the most beautiful villa I have seen". Destroyed by fire in 1888, it now only remains in name.

In the New King's Road, the old coach route that led to Putney Heath, stands the original pottery kiln founded by John Dwight. The pottery itself is long gone.

In 1877, on the sight of Seagrove Road, the Fulham Smallpox Hospital was built. During its erection, there was a stipulation that no building occupied by patients should be within a 100 feet of the nearby Butcher's Alms houses in Walham Green. Today, on the site of the pox hospital and the retired meat-trade cottages, stands a gleaming block of luxury apartments with swimming pool, underground parking, fancy shrubs and a clutch of BMWs, Jaguars and Volvo estates.

And Fulham, like so many other central London districts, took a pounding during the Blitz. The first bomb fell at 3a.m. on 9th September 1940 at 132 St. Dunstan's Road. Several people died. Next came the Fulham Hospital and the turbine house at the local power station. Other targets were around Olympia where the marshalling yards were located and, of course, the gas works. My own street, Hestercombe

Avenue, had two houses destroyed by high explosives and several others damaged by incendiary bombs.

The last bomb to fall on Fulham was in fact a V2 rocket which hit Beaumont Crescent on 2nd August 1944.

This memoire is about Fulham in the 1940s and 1950s, a time of both austerity and change, of ration books and dance halls, of Teddy Boys and hope and innocence and wonderment and disillusion and the tangy bustle of street life in SW6.

The reminiscences that follow are not meant to be a historical journey or an architectural reflection or even a sociological study. They are just tales prompted by my memory of things past, the raucous vigour of the North End Road market, the great plane trees in Bishop's Park, the views across the River Thames to faraway Putney.

They might, I hope, paint a brief portrait of life in this corner of a great city seen through the eyes of a young boy when London was recovering from the second of the great wars of the turbulent 20th century.

My parents were not Londoners. Both of them were born in Wiltshire, Father in a village called Hanging Langford, Mother in Salisbury. They came to London shortly after their marriage in the 1920s when Father joined the Metropolitan Police in that time of high unemployment. A job in the police force was secure, safe and pensionable. Father stayed in the force for 25 years and he and Mother both lived, and subsequently died, in Fulham.

For me, it was the place I grew up, where I went to primary school, where I played in the streets, where my education was gained as much in those streets as it was at my subsequent grammar school. It was where I was first kissed, first had fumbled sex, first experienced unrequited love, first felt stirrings of ambition and first realised just how extraordinarily lucky I was to be born in London, in the greatest city in the world.

The Rhythm Of Life

The rhythm of life has changed in Fulham. Although it was always a busy place, in the 1940s people seemed less driven, more in control of their daily lives. People still queued for buses but, unlike today, were not constantly glancing at their watches in an agitated manner or yelling fatuities down mobile phones.

The unfolding early morning pageant in our street was of front doors opening, milk bottles being picked up by women in dressing gowns, their hair in curlers; of men in macs with Trilby hats, clutching lunch packages, walking briskly towards Fulham Road and the buses; of children in school uniform, satchels slung over their shoulders, caps awry, walking snail-like towards Munster Road.

Dogs, usually skinny terriers, would be barking and urinating against the cast iron lamp posts while Owen the milk was pulling his handcart loaded with empty bottles before returning to the dairy at Waldemar. He'd have been on duty delivering milk since 6 a.m.

Once a week, there would be the clip-clop of the coalman's horse and soon the huge animal with its leather and brass harness would stand outside our house while sacks of coal were manhandled off the cart and emptied into the coal-hole.

Men would glide past on bicycles. There were no cars in Hestercombe Avenue, no sound of motors being started, engines roaring, doors being slammed. You could actually hear birds singing in the few trees people had planted in their tiny gardens. No aeroplanes screamed or droned overhead. Heathrow was still a heath.

The local sweep arrived on a bike with his brushes and paraphernalia strapped in a sack on his back like a quiver full of arrows. He was a truly theatrical sweep, his face always jet black, teeth bright and white, a big cloth cap worn rakishly on his curly head. He looked like a sweep should. He dressed the part. It was considered lucky to touch the sweep if you saw him, but I never dared to. He came to my sister's wedding, by arrangement, so she could kiss him for good luck after the ceremony. He turned up in his full gear, brushes, black face, cap, bucket and of course his bike.

My policeman father, if he wasn't on night duty, would mount his bike at the kerb, wearing a mac over his police uniform, his helmet concealed in the saddle bag, and cycle off to Victoria where his station was located.

The woman across the road had a fetish about shaking rugs out of an upper-storey window, which task she performed daily, showering passers by with clouds of dust and other flotsam. I could never understand why her rugs needed such regular attention. It could have been the mess created by her five cats and two dogs.

Although it had been many years since the knife grinder toured the street with his stone grinding wheel mounted on the front of his bike, we still had the rag and bone man, a man of ancient years, back bent like a bow, pushing a handcart with peeling yellow paint. His cry, which pierced the early morning air, was "ragbottleanbone". He collected very few bones in 1946, but rags and bottles in abundance. I've often wondered what he did with them all.

The local dustmen, too, patrolled the streets pushing their dustcarts. They had huge brushes with long wooden handles, and shovels to remove rotting fruit, horse manure and other detritus. They dressed like Dick Van Dyke in *Mary Poppins*. cloth caps, string around the trousers below the knee, big boots and spotted handkerchiefs round their throats. And they were proud to be called dustmen. Not roadsweepers or municipal street orderlies. Cheerful men with ruddy, lined faces and voices like gravel sliding over slate. The job with the council was a job for life.

Round the corner from our street, in Fulham Road, the shops opened early. The butcher stood on his step, arms folded, striped apron around his waist, straw hat tilted back on his head. Behind him hung headless cows, gutted pigs with their trotters tied together, unplucked chickens, strings of sausages and dishes of liver, tripe, kidneys and gruesome great tongues that just lay on the slabs, all pink and grey and covered in what looked like pimples or goose bumps.

The number 14 bus would swing into Fulham Road from its starting point in distant Putney and stop outside the chemist's. It was here that denizens of Fulham could make the journey through Chelsea and South Kensington and Knightsbridge to Piccadilly and then beyond to Hackney Wick, a place so far away, so alien, it might as well have been Timbuctoo.

Bus conductors on the number 14 seemed to know everybody at every stop along the way. As the bus chuntered by the chemist's shop at the start of the Fulham Road, the conductor would shout his greetings and urge people to "move on down inside", or utter the famous injunction, "plenty of room on top".

An insurance salesman of my father's acquaintance who lived in Waldemar Avenue was one of the first in our area to buy one of the new Morris Minors, £569 in 1948, more than a year's wages for many people. A nervous driver, this fellow! He would try to pull out behind the 14 bus as it moved away from the bus stop, and then, with his pork pie hat rammed over his head, he would follow the bus all the way to South Kensington where his office was located.

Local cynics claimed the man must be on the fiddle. I mean to say, a new Morris Minor, at £569: how many honest working men had that kind of money?

When the Minor was first launched, the owner of Morris Motors, Lord Nuffield, said he thought it was horrible, "like a poached egg". Well, egg or not, poached, fried or otherwise, it became one of the longest-lasting and most popular cars of the century.

Late afternoon would see a subtle change of pace in Fulham life: young mothers in long woollen coats, pushing prams to Bishop's Park and often snatching a drag at a Woodbine as they walked; window cleaners on bikes, balancing long ladders and buckets, moving through their afternoon appointments; young children drifting home from school, the girls chattering and giggling, the boys kicking a frayed tennis ball along the gutter or using their satchels like flails to assault their companions.

Mrs. Collier's lame dog, Rexy, limping alongside the children and barking in a high-pitched falsetto; Mrs. Bailey, our upstairs neighbour, flinging open her window and turning her wireless up to full volume; Doris Day singing "Buttons and Bows".

The newspaper seller would be at the corner of Munster and Fulham roads with his stacks of *Evening News, Star* and *Standard*. Three evening papers, a cornucopia of news for Londoners in 1949, while across the road from our house, there's Mrs. Little opening her *Evening News* while she stands on her front doorstep and reads items aloud to nobody in particular. "Ooh," she exclaims, "Terence Rattigan's got a new play out, *The Browning Version*".

Opposite, the tiny, wrinkled figure of a female Methuselah called Miss Salt stiffens. "Brownies what?" she screeches and then, sotto voice, "Stuck up cow. Oo's she tryin' to impress?"

Dusk. And a cool wind is blowing off the Thames. Street lights are coming on, glowing softly in the gathering gloom. Although we are a mile from the river, you can hear the throaty honk of a tugboat as it passes under Putney Bridge.

Down at Walham Green and in the North End Road, the street traders are stacking merchandise into boxes and taking the tarpaulin covers off their barrows. Some have big leather satchels tied round their waists, bulging with coins. Most don't have bank accounts and deal only in cash. The street is knee deep in waste paper, half-eaten fruit, cigarette butts and pieces of string.

The Fulham Borough Council's roadsweepers, the dustmen, will soon tackle these mounds of rubbish. One famous fellow, still working at 67, called Roddy, whistles while he works and people marvel at his shrill tones. "He's another Ronnie Renalde," they cry. But he's not. He's just a cheerful dustman, doing his job, the same job he's done for 52 years.

They are pulling down the blinds at Frost's, the big grocers in Fulham Road, and the lady librarian from Fulham Library is pulling on her woollen gloves as she leaves the building. It's been a busy day; several people have borrowed copies of "George Orwell's *1984*. The librarian has read it herself. The future, she concludes, doesn't sound too rosy.

Mr. Gear alights from the number 4 bus outside the chemist's. He is wearing a pearl-grey Homburg, leather gloves and a silver tie with a shiny tiepin. He has spent the day as hairdresser at Whites Club in St. James's and cut the hair of two earls, a duke and an admiral. Tonight he will eat egg and chips from a plastic table in his tiny kitchen. After he has finished, he will put the coins he received as tips at Whites into a large pottery jar. His wife, the frail Mrs. Gear, will make him a cup of tea and after listening to the BBC news on the wireless at nine o'clock, they will go to bed in their bedroom which has lino, not carpet, on the floor.

Jack Bailey, the park keeper, who lives upstairs in Hestercombe with his wife, Mad Kate, is loping home from Bishop's Park in his blue uniform with little crowns on the lapels and carrying his pointy stick which he uses to spear leaves. He is an avuncular Geordie with a large, moon-shaped face. As he approaches Hestercombe, his wife shouts at him from the upstairs window. "Jack," she yells, eyes gleaming behind wire-framed glasses, "Jack, I had tea today with Queen Victoria."

Jack shrugs as he passes my mother on the front step. He knows his wife is loopy. He is a patient, tolerant man. He acknowledges my mother with a rueful smile. "She's 'armless," he says, "no 'arm in 'er at all." Mum nods. Kate is eccentric, occasionally very noisy, but without a bad bone in her body.

Across the road, Mrs. Wootton with her swan-like neck and fur trimmed hat is gazing into the middle distance waiting for her son, Desmond, who has been, and will be, eleven years old for ever, to come home from visiting a friend.

In most of the houses in Hestercombe, the evening meal is being prepared. It is not called dinner. Many doors have been left ajar to greet returning husbands or children. There have been no burglaries in Hestercombe for donkey's years. Why should there be? There isn't much to steal.

Apart from Grandfather's dress sword.

The day is winding down. The streets are quiet, but you can still hear the odd sparrow chirping. Rexy, the limping dog, shuffles past, a little bell tinkling on his collar.

It's time for his evening meal too.

Village Life

Fulham in the 1940s, with its streets of terraced Edwardian and Victorian houses, was primarily working class. There were enclaves of bourgeois respectability on the fringes of Hurlingham, close by the Thames and alongside Bishop's Park, where stood rows of pretty villas with stained glass panels above their doors and clipped privet hedges to the front.

However, the north end of Fulham was decidedly rough with mean streets and grim tenements built by philanthropists like Lord Shaftesbury or the Guinness Trust.

The invisible *cordon sanitaire* that separated Fulham from Bohemian Chelsea and quasi-rural Putney was the River Thames on one side and the small bridge over the railway line by Chelsea football ground in Fulham Road.

In our part of Fulham, the large, three-storey Edwardian villas had once been single family homes for successful merchants and the emerging business class. By the mid-1930s and after the Second World War, they were converted mostly into flats for that curious section of society, often patronisingly referred to as the 'respectable' working class: foremen, policemen, inspectors on the buses, men who carried clipboards to work

16

and wore macs with belts and Trilby hats that looked like pork pies. Cloth caps, the standard headgear of the proletariat, were frowned upon in our neck of the woods and were only sighted when you reached the environs of Walham Green.

The cluster of streets off the Fulham Road and north of the Thames had something of a village feel about them. Front doors were left open in summer and there was much social intercourse over the walls of the tiny back yards or front steps.

Although close to the open space and field of Bishop's Park, which I frequented throughout my childhood, most children still played in the streets: ancient rituals, unchanged from the 19th century, like hopscotch, knock-down-ginger, marbles, street football, ring-a-ring of roses, skipping.

We knew all the local traders as nobody went further than the corner shop for their basic provisions. Mr. Brown, the tobacconist, in Fulham Road, sold my father Player's Navy Cut, plastic sachets of lighter fuel, pipes and Swan Vesta matches. Smoking and its attendant rituals were a big deal in Fulham in the 1940s.

The shelves of Mr. Brown's shop were crammed with every conceivable brand of cigarette, even the exotic Passing Cloud in their pink boxes and evil-smelling Egyptian fags with a picture of a man in a Fez on the packet.

Owen the milkman, a genial balding Welshman with a wholly undeserved reputation as a ladies' man, had a small, old-fashioned dairy on the corner of Waldemar and Lalor streets. Big churns of milk would be delivered to the dairy from heavy lorries and Owen would fill milk bottles from them with a steel ladle, seal the tops with a cardboard lid, load them onto his wooden cart and hand-deliver them door-to-door.

In Owen's shop, which had a marble counter, butter would be slapped into brick shapes with wooden paddles. There was also a large porcelain cow of gender clash expression which stood proudly at one end of the counter. It had magnificent curving horns and huge pink udders which caused me and other young lads endless amusement. I once bet Johnny Plant sixpence that he wouldn't fondle the cow's ceramic nipples when we were in the shop on errands for our respective mothers.

Johnny took up the challenge, but unfortunately Mr. Owen spotted him in mid-grope and whacked him on the head with a butter paddle.

Coal was delivered by horse and cart in our streets too. Great sacks of the stuff would be heaved from the back of the cart by young helpers with black faces and leather waistcoats, How I envied them. The sacks would be up-ended into your coal-hole; all our houses had cellars, and it would slide down the chute with a satisfying swoosh, sending up a cloud of fine coal dust that would settle on the front step later to be swept up by mothers in aprons and headscarves.

During the operation of coal delivery, it was not uncommon for the huge carthorse to take a monumental crap in the road. Almost by a process of clairvoyance, householders knew this had happened and would rush out clutching dustpans and little shovels to gather up the precious manure. Back gardens were tiny, but many people grew tomatoes or tiny rose bushes on their scrap of earth and it was a holy ritual to keep them well fed.

For some years, I was highly suspicious of tomatoes because I erroneously concluded that when Father said manure was good for them, he was planning to sprinkle horse-droppings over them at the table during our meal.

In Fulham during the 1940s, men worked and the women stayed at home. Maintaining a household in the days before washing machines or spin driers or other labour-saving devices, was a hard, even arduous, task. Our small, two-bedroom flat seemed to require a staggering amount of activity from my mother to keep it spick and span.

As there were no fitted carpets, linoleum surrounds had to be polished twice a week. Coal fires created dust and ash and needed cleaning out daily. Front steps needed to be washed and mopped, grates needed blacking, floors "Hoovered" with a manual cleaner, windows polished, furniture waxed and then there was laundry — mountains of the stuff. God knows where it all came from. None of us had a lot of clothes, but sets of heavy blankets, sheets and pillowcases had to be washed by hand, scrubbed and pummelled in galvanised zinc baths full of hot, sudsy water, then squeezed through a mangle with wooden rollers in the tiny back yard and finally hung with wooden pegs in the even tinier garden.

Ladies "things" — my sister's knickers, Mum's slip, bras and cotton frocks — were dried inside the house in front of the fire on a wooden clothes horse.

The preparation of food was a gigantic task, three hot meals a day all rustled up in a scullery that was no bigger than a closet: stone-floored with a huge ceramic sink and brass taps that spurted and gurgled and a gas cooker with blackened rings above which, on a narrow shelf, were stacked an array of huge, dented saucepans and a frying pan with a handle wrapped in string. Under the sink was a metal tray which contained vegetables — potatoes, carrots, greens, loose peas — while meat, a must at all meals, was kept on a plate in the cellar or in a tin cupboard outside in the yard. How Mother managed to create such substantial feasts from this chaotic jumble remains one of life's unsolved mysteries.

Breakfast was always cooked: bacon, eggs, sausages, toast, hot tea — never coffee — and marmalade. When Dad was on police duty, I've seen him eat five eggs and six rashers of streaky bacon plus two pints of tea so strong it would strip the gold paint off the Albert Memorial.

Most meals included mashed potatoes which had been cooked with great knobs of butter and lots of salt. Mother's other vegetables were always boiled to death and we would crush the already soggy carrots or peas into the heap of potatoes before smothering the resultant blob with brown sauce or tomato ketchup.

Bread was cut in traditional doorstep slices and also plastered with butter or, occasionally during rationing, butter mixed with lard or margarine.

There were no bananas during the war and I didn't even see one until I was ten years old. There were dried substitutes that could be obtained, dark brown, crescent shaped things that resembled dog turds that had been left out in the sun.

Through the distorting prism of nearly 60 years, it now seems that my mother's life then was dominated by food and laundry. There were no hobbies, no housewives' coffee mornings or sewing circles, no theatre visits, at least none until my sister became a singer and went on the stage. Dad's work as a policeman involved long, often unsocial, hours and on days off, he was too tired for more than just the occasional outing: a bus ride to Putney Heath perhaps or a walk in the park. I don't think either Mum or Dad saw the inside of a restaurant until they were in their 50s.

Nobody owned a car in our neck of Fulham except the landlord. Today, each street is crammed bumper to bumper with gleaming metal, at least two per household, often more.

Bicycles of course proliferated — ancient machines with big baskets on the handlebars, low-slung racing jobs for the aristocrats of labour like Glen the son of Owen the milkman. My father rode a sturdy BSA with a huge saddle bag all the way from Fulham to the police station at which he served in Victoria, every working day of his life.

I had a red Norman Invader bicycle for my twelfth birthday, second-hand of course, but still a touch daring, something of a bird-puller in the 1940s. Helen, my girl friend, used to sit on the cross bar and lean back against me as I pedalled. I'm here to tell you that this was an erotic experience undreamt of even by the authors of the *Arabian Nights*.

Insurance was collected door to door by a man on a bike who wore bicycle clips and carried a battery of fountain pens in his top pocket. Mother paid a bob a week, but just what she was insuring, I was never able to ascertain. The insurance man would scribble in his little book, acknowledging the collection of each shilling and then put a big tick next to our name, like a schoolteacher marking homework.

Some years later, after I'd joined the army, I learnt that the insurance man's brother was a local undertaker. A very crafty arrangement when you come to think about it. If it were indeed life insurance Mother was paying for, then even if a customer snuffed it and the insurance company had to pay out, the brother could clip you for the cost of a funeral.

Nobody had a telephone. In fact, the instrument was considered a rather sinister thing as people only tended to use the public phone box when they had bad news to impart. My mother hated the telephone and, years later, when I had one installed in her flat, she would often leave it off the hook as she disliked the noise it made when it rang. Curiously, my mother's voice on the telephone sounded quite different from her normal speech. Even though she'd lived in Fulham for over twenty years, the telephone brought out her rich Wiltshire brogue.

Both my parents preferred verbal communication, as did most of our friends and neighbours in Fulham. The gossipy chat over a garden fence or the exchange of news on the front doorstep were most favoured locations. Pubs, of course, were also popular venues for socialising, although I cannot recall either of my parents' ever going to a pub even though Fulham had literally dozens.

Mother was a great believer in written communication too. Although she had left school at the age of thirteen, she could write fluently and legibly all her life. She liked leaving little notes around the house. These were often instructions to my father, my sister and me. "Cheese on cellar stairs". "Don't use mangle — handle broken". Clean socks on line in kitchen'. And one I particularly remember was a stern injunction to my father, "Don't forget to brush your hat."

I should have kept them. There must have been hundreds of them scribbled on tiny scraps of paper over the years.

On Saturdays, "big shopping" took place at the North End Road Market, one of scores that London boasted during the 1950s. The street was lined both sides with barrows selling everything from fruit and vegetables to gentlemen's hats. My father once spotted Mr. Gear, our neighbour who was a hairdresser at Whites Club up West, buying a pearl-grey Homburg in the North End Road Market. "He lashed out two quid for that hat," said my father in a tone of incredulity. For years afterwards, I assumed that anybody who purchased a hat for two pounds was as rich as Croesus.

The market was a microcosm of working-class life in London. It was noisy, crowded and exuberant. The barrow boys were the great entrepreneurs of the 1950s, living on their wits and their brilliant salesmanship.

Today, we have quasi-academic courses in "marketing" and "communication skills" and a lot of guff about "unique selling propositions" (USP) or "squeezing the emotional buying trigger" (EBT). There is even a degree course in "media and communication". The barrow boys in North End Road would have laughed at this pretentious nonsense. They knew instinctively how to make the proposition — engage your interest, whet your appetite and close the sale. Slam, bam and thank you ma'am.

They could sell anything: jars of pickled onions, alarm clocks, hand-painted neckties, boxes of candied fruit, wax crucifixes, plimsolls (an ancestor of the trainer), fruit, vegetables, army helmets, teddy bears, china dolls, tartan waistcoats, balls of string bigger than a football, tin cups, glass vases, boxes of soap suds, umbrellas, second-hand soccer boots, fire irons and bamboo screens hand-painted in the Forbidden City by Mandarin craftsmen — "never mind about five quid madam, I gotta be going crazy, I'm giving it away madam, but to you not even four quid, or bloody three. Who wants it? Two pound ten. Blimey madam, you'll take three. God bless you."

One particular barrow boy specialised in tubs of Brylcreem, combs, brushes and hand mirrors. There were always a cluster of lads around his stall stocking up on these vital items. Big Georgie Hughes whose mum had a second-hand furniture shop at Walham Green said that this bloke could also obtain contraceptives if you so desired. In those days, young scruffs like myself called them by a most inelegant name, spunk bladders. I never actually saw this barrow boy sell a contraceptive, but Georgie Hughes was very streetwise. If he'd told me you could buy elephant sweat in bottles from the barrow, I'd have believed him.

One of my very favourite shops in Fulham was the bread and dripping shop in the Fulham Road dangerously close to the Chelsea border where toffs and wankers resided.

Perhaps I should explain. I once heard my father describing the denizens of Chelsea in these terms. Toffs and wankers. Today, the phrase sounds like a theme pub.

Anyway, the bread and dripping shop was so small that it was almost a cupboard, just a hole in the wall really. It sold loose sweets from big glass jars, striped humbugs, toffees, hunks of fudge and counterfeit liquorice allsorts, but its major trade was in bread and dripping. Great slices of white bread smothered in beef fat and liberally salted at a penny a slice. Its customers were mostly schoolboys from nearby Sloane School in Hortensia Road. A penny a slice, but you could get three slices for tuppence. A feast of cholesterol fit for the gods.

There is no meal I have consumed, before or since, that could hold a candle to eating three doorstep-thick slices of bread and dripping while sauntering along Fulham Road in the rain, and not wearing your school cap.

Oh yes, we laughed in the face of danger then, risking both cardiac arrest and disciplinary action from Sloane School prefects who regarded boys without caps as dangerous miscreants.

My idea of an afterlife, in Heaven, is sitting on a cloud and consuming endless slices of bread and dripping, perhaps accompanied by celestial trumpets. As long as God's little helpers know that the secret of perfect bread and dripping is the soaking of the bread in blood gravy before slapping on the dollops of beef fat. It's a specialised form of culinary expertise.

I suppose Heaven has a bit of that knocking about up there. If it doesn't, then I'm not going.

Shops

Mr. Shepherd's shop was situated at the junction of Fulham Road and Fulham Palace Road. It was more of a corridor than a shop, with bare, scrubbed floorboards and a long counter of wood and marble. Open sacks of rice and dried peas and cereals were stacked along the wall, leaving less than two feet for customers to wriggle past. At one end of the counter was a bacon-slicing machine, all gleaming steel and a softly whirring wheel that cut meat into miraculously thin pieces. Behind the counter were shelves, packed to the ceiling with tins of beans and soup and condensed milk and packets of tea. Mr. Shepherd was thin, with an Adam's apple that wobbled as he spoke. He always wore a light brown coat and kept a pencil behind his ear. His wife, who helped in the shop, was prematurely grey and wore her hair 1920s style in neatly waved discs over each ear.

Mr. Shepherd was the world's best adder-up. He used to jot down all the items you had bought, in pencil, on the counter and then, to the amazement of all those in the shop, run his pencil down the side of the column, and presto! The total. He never made a mistake. For him to see a list which included prices like 12/6 1/2d, 4/9d, 17/6d, 8/6 1/2d, 11/4 3/4d was chicken feed to Mr. Shepherd. The world's greatest adder-up.

He would also cut coupons from Mum's ration book with a huge pair of scissors and his mouth would make a cutting movement as he snipped away. Sometimes he allowed Mum more eggs than she was entitled to and didn't always snip all the coupons.

That was because she had a growing boy. Me. Mr. Shepherd had two cats to keep down the mice. One of them was half-bald through fighting and would turn its back on you in a haughty fashion and raise its tail revealing a small pink bum-hole.

My most vivid memory of Mr. Shepherd's shop is of his adding up figures at high speed and slicing paper-thin pieces of bacon or pouring loose rice into packets with a wooden shovel while the cat with the bald head turned round and showed you its little pink bumhole, haughtily.

Mrs. Shepherd liked to keep her eye on the tins of biscuits that were stacked high against the wall. All the tins had wonderful pictures on the lid, usually of the King and Queen and one, I remember, of Winston Churchill looking pink and young in officer's uniform.

Mrs. Shepherd had to keep an eye on those tins because it was not unknown for boys to prise up their lids and palm a chocolate digestive when the shop was busy.

Mum didn't often send me shopping, but when she did, I knew that Mrs. Shepherd would give me a biscuit before I left so I never had to nick one, ever.

Just along the road from Shepherd's the grocer, was a sweet shop, that is to say, a shop that specialised exclusively in confectionery and chocolate. To a child, it was something of an Aladdin's Cave with its big jars of loose boiled sweets and its shelves of chocolate bars and marzipan, as well as toffees, humbugs, soft jelly babies in various colours, sticks of liquorice and liquorice "boot laces", milk chocolate in commercial packages and one of my favourites, loose hunks of chocolate in big glass jars that would be weighed out on a set of brass scales and shovelled into a paper bag, twisted shut and handed to you for sixpence.

The chunks were enormous — of jaw-dislocating size — some studded with nuts, others with fat dried raisins, and always a mixture of creamy milk chocolate and the bitter, dark plain variety.

There was toffee in slabs a foot long that snapped in half with a sharp report when you could only afford half a piece, marzipan spheres the size of a large marble, lemon sherbet sold in waxed cylindrical packets, candied fruit, oval cough drops so hot they made your eyes water, peppermints like pennies, chewing gums, some plain others coated with a crisp shell of sugar.

And huge boxes of chocolates tied with red or blue ribbons — fabulous exotic collections, some of which were the size of small table tops. These were for special occasions. Men with guilty expressions and macs with the collars turned up would buy them to placate wronged or angry wives. Or mistresses.

The sweet shop was run by two elderly ladies, both of whom were thin as rails. They obviously didn't consume their profits. They were sharp, cockney women who would sell "broken" chocolate to us kids at knock-down prices and whatever we purchased, they would always throw in something extra for nothing, a stick of liquorice, a small slab of toffee.

I was also fond of the general store in Fulham Road which was a miraculous jumble of every household item conceivable. It was a big shop with polished floorboards and a long counter around which were stocked brooms, dustpans, kettles, balls of twine, cartons of matches, tins of paraffin, loose nails, screws, sink plungers, plugs, light-bulbs, batteries, bird seed, dog food, hooks, door handles, floor polish, dishcloths, scouring pads, mops, buckets, pails, brown paper, rolls of lino, wallpaper paste, dog collars, oil heaters, brass door knockers, giant scissors, sets of carving knives, tins of lighter fuel, wooden ladders, doormats, curtain rails, puncture repair outfits, rolls of waxed paper, car jacks, fire tongs, coal scuttles and, most miraculous of all to me at least, tiny bottles of oil with a rubber dropper inside the lid for loosening ear wax.

Just how the family who ran this extraordinary general store knew what they had in their inventory amazed me. They seemed able to supply anything, on demand, and were never out of stock.

The shop had a curious fascination for me. To begin with, it had its own particular smell, a combination of linseed oil and floor polish and wood shavings and it was always full of customers making purchases of staggering variety.

The father and son behind the counter, cheerful, smiling, never harassed, knew just where everything was, from a box of matches to a mangle with wooden rollers. All sales were rung up on the usual brass cash register and all transactions were of course in ready money, although tick was available to selected customers.

Such stores have all but disappeared now although I saw something close to it in the 1980s in Atlanta, Georgia, U.S.A. It was regarded as an eccentric novelty. I thought it was wonderful.

School

My father was keen for me to obtain a good education, "a vital key to life" was the way he described it. I think his enthusiasm for my academic progress was in part influenced by his own experience in Wiltshire when he was a boy. His education at a small village school was curtailed when he was seventeen and he joined the Royal Engineers to fight in the Great War. It was 1915 and, urged on by his father, my grandad, ex-Quartermaster Sergeant Frank Turner of the King's Royal Rifles, he lied about his age and was soon on a troopship bound for France.

I think that years later, while proud to have served in uniform for his country, he regretted not going to university where, he claimed, he would have read engineering.

I'm inclined to believe, however, that English or history would have been his proper subjects; he was an avid and sophisticated reader with a sharp, creative imagination. What he lacked however, was self-confidence and ambition. I inherited those from my mother who once warned me that the dividing line between self-confidence and arrogance was a very thin one, a remarkably astute observation from a woman who had left school at the age of thirteen to help raise her six brothers in Salisbury.

At primary school in Sherbrooke Road, Fulham, I was taught by the remarkable, avuncular Mr. Downey, a man who could alone capture and hold the interest of a bunch of scrofulous, noisy, working-class children who looked upon school as a hated chore. Later I took my eleven-plus.

To me and most of my friends in Fulham, this was a most crucial moment in our lives although few of us realised it at the time. Failure to pass the eleven-plus meant being sent to a "comprehensive" or "secondary modern" school where the education was more technical and trade oriented than academic.

Even in the 1940s, going to the local "secondary" meant you had failed one of life's early hurdles. But I passed, to the unconcealed joy of my parents, and was sent to the Sloane Grammar School in Chelsea, a splendid establishment where the masters wore gowns and the curriculum mimicked that of the best public schools.

Here at Sloane, although it may sound gruesomely and politically incorrect to state it today, the objective of the educational process was to turn working-class children into middle-class citizens. Base metal into gold, or as cynics might put it, sows' ears into silk purses.

But in the early 1940s, grammar school entrants came from a variety of backgrounds. More than a few had public school-educated parents who couldn't afford school fees for their offspring and one or two were actually sons of the impoverished nobility, plus a few brilliant immigrants like my brother-in-law who had left Budapest with his parents to escape the threat of Nazism and, at the age of six, arrived in England without a word of English. He subsequently became a Master of Science in engineering. Sloane School was therefore a remarkable social minestrone, an eclectic mix of backgrounds and even races, although predominately white Anglo-Saxon. The common denominator was the fact that all the boys at Sloane had secured their places on merit. School uniform, which was compulsory, further added to the sense of "togetherness" and helped to soften any distinctions that might arise from the boys' varied backgrounds.

The masters at Sloane, on the whole, were a remarkable bunch ranging from dour academics like the chemistry master, Mr. Middleditch, to the wonderfully elegant and brilliant Mr. Berkeley. One of the French masters, a dusty Falstaffian figure called Harry Little, organised my first ever visit to France, where he enhanced our love of foreign languages by taking a bunch of us, aged twelve, to Monmartre to witness a large lady of uncertain age dance on a platform with a mirrored floor without any knickers on. Anatomy and French grammar all in one wonderful lesson.

In my early days at Sloane, I remember standing in the playground with a chum from primary school, Bill Marsden, wearing our new grey shorts, blazers and caps and looking up at the large forbidding pile that was Sloane School. Just across the road and beyond the high school walls was the Chelsea football ground, and to the right along the Fulham Road was dazzlingly, sophisticated South Kensington and a little further through Knightsbridge was the West End.

Oh yes, Bill and I agreed, we had certainly arrived. Here we were at a grammar school in Chelsea, having crossed that invisible rubicon at Stamford Bridge which separated it from Fulham. Bill and I were discussing the various masters at the school and assessing which ones we thought were "O.K." and which ones were "rotten". There was no middle way, they were either O.K. or rotten.

"Lumsdaine is O.K.," I ventured.

Bill took a bite from his egg sandwich weighing this verdict.

"He's Australian," he said

"Yes," I replied, "but he's still O.K."

Bill chewed the mouthful carefully. "But he teaches English."

I nodded. "Yeah, but he's a good teacher."

And he was. A sunburned, bald Australian with a pronounced Queensland drawl but a splendid master who once wrote on my report, "Turner's written work is excellent in all respects." Maybe that's why I thought he was O.K. His manner of speaking was in direct contrast to many of the other masters who spoke in carefully modulated, public school tones.

The headmaster, Guy Boas, spoke like an 18th-century aristocrat. He uttered phrases like, "keep 'orf' the grass" and "how frightfully boring". He was also, I learnt subsequently, the librarian of the famous Garrick

Club in London, which I joined over half a century later.

The quality of the teaching at Sloane was, on the whole, very good. I was never drawn to the science subjects however, as the masters who took them tended to be rather dull. I enjoyed experiments in chemistry, as most boys do, but was rebuked for constantly demanding lessons in the making of explosives. "Turner," the dour Mr. Middleditch said to me once, "there is more to chemistry, boy, than blowing things up."

There was no part of the curriculum that attempted to manipulate our social attitudes or force upon us any kind of political dogma. It is probably fair to say that the general thrust of opinion at Sloane was right of centre, a sort of mild conservatism with a small "c". Nobody was encouraged to suffer pangs of post-imperial guilt and elitism was not yet a dirty word.

One master, a Mr. Selman, had been an RAF Wing Commander during the war and presented a dashing, heroic figure to us thirteen year olds. He actually used words like "prang" and "wizard" and "topnotch" just like the fictional characters in "champion" comics. Indeed, it was rumoured darkly in the corridors of Sloane, that Selman was the very man upon whom Rockfist Rogan RAF had been modelled.

Right next door to Sloane School, in Hortensia Road, Chelsea, was a girls' school, Carlyle, a girls' grammar. If you stood on another boys' shoulders, you could look over the wall and see the girls in the warm weather doing PT in their blue knickers and white shirts. Some of them had better legs than Betty Grable. Most didn't though. If it was a windy day, the girls' legs looked like Spam.

I enjoyed Sloane, although looking back I wish I'd worked harder. I joined the school Shakespeare Society and played Salanio in *The Merchant of Venice*. I wrote precociously sophisticated articles for the school magazine, *The Cheynean*; I played soccer at outside left for the First XI, and I represented the school in the 100 yards and 220 yards at White City in the London Grammar Schools' Competition. My long jump of 18 1/2 feet at sixteen in school sports remained unbroken for many years.

With National Service looming at age eighteen, I put aside any thoughts of going on to university, a decision that I regret most of all.

Towards the end of my time at Sloane, I had a meeting with the headmaster, Guy Boas, to discuss my future. His room was panelled and had a vase of flowers on the desk. He lit an Oval cigarette and paced up and down, his gown flapping, talking in his high-pitched, upper-class voice. His white moustache was tinged with nicotine and his dental work was later copied by Harold Macmillan, the Prime Minister. "You're not doing very well in maths," he said, "or chemistry or physics." This was true, I was not of the slightest scientific bent. "But," continued Boas, exhaling Turkish cigarette smoke in a fine jet from between pursed lips, "you are doing well in English."

"And art," I said.

"Yes," said Boas, a cloud of perfumed smoke hanging above his head.

"And history," I said.

"Yes, yes, yes," said Boas crossly. He hated being interrupted.

"I like writing," I said, standing my ground.

"Yes," said Boas, "and Mr. Lumsdaine says you have an extremely agile imagination."

"I'm good at geography too," I said, a touch bolder.

"Alright, Turner," Boas said, "let's not continue the catalogue of your academic achievements." He crushed out his cigarette in a large green ashtray and immediately lit another, the match flaring as he struck it.

For a moment, he seemed to disappear behind a cloud of smoke, then he coughed and walked over to his window. I thought this was a gesture of dismissal, but he turned and smiled, a sort of patrician grimace. "You must learn to speak," he said. "Do you understand?"

"Speak?" I said, mystified. That's all I had been doing.

"Properly," said Boas. "You must learn to speak as well as you write. You spoke Shakespeare's verse very well in *The Merchant*. You must do it in the course of everyday life. Learn to speak and write English really well. Really well, Turner." Then he paused and took a contemplative pull at his cigarette. "I shouldn't perhaps be saying this Turner," he continued, "but don't worry too much about the maths. When you leave school, other people will do the sums for you. The English language is the most powerful artillery a man can have in this world."

"Yes," I said, delighted, "Yes Sir. Absolutely."

It was the best advice I've ever had. Somebody's always done the maths for me ever since.

Art Attack

Our art master at Sloane School in Chelsea cut a striking figure. He had whitish hair and a thick, black moustache not unlike Gilbert Roland, the Mexican Hollywood actor. His name was Mr. Smart and he wore daring sports jackets in bold checks and loosely knotted ties, and, as my friend Bill Marsden once said, "He could draw like fuck."

And he could. Art was always an enjoyable period in the school curriculum. I found I had a crude skill in cartoon-like drawings and a total lack of skill in painting.

"Open your eyes," Mr. Smart used to say. "There is art all around us. In buildings, in the curve of a church spire, in the shape of a bus even."

Once, when I was about fourteen, Mr. Smart took a group of us up to the West End to visit what he described as the "best of London's art galleries". This was in 1949 for God's sake.

So with our eyes wide open, we all piled into a London bus, a number 14, and travelled up to Piccadilly where, once decanted under the imposing figure of Eros, Mr. Smart led us in a crocodile to the Royal Academy, the National and a couple of places in Jermyn Street I can't remember.

What I do remember, because they are imprinted indelibly in my mind, are some of the spectacular pictures we saw that day. I recall standing in front of Bronzino's fabulous painting, *An Allegory with Venus and Cupid*. For sheer, trouser-splitting eroticism, this took the biscuit. Stunning, magical, utterly sensational. A completely naked Venus is being caressed by Cupid as his ruby lips brush hers. His right hand cups her left breast and between his fingers, one sees her erect nipple.

It was enough to blow my brains out.

Acquired by the National Gallery in 1860, it is widely accepted as the most erotic painting in the entire collection. Venus has a modern figure, slim, athletic, narrow waisted and she's shaved her pubic hair. Or, as Mr. Smart said roguishly, somebody had. I stood there in a welter of lust and awe. Lust at the sheer sexuality of the image and awe at the technical perfection of the painting.

Still tingling from the effect of Bronzino's masterpiece, Mr. Smart marched us into another high-ceilinged room to see the monumental oil by Rubens of Samson and Delilah. This is a huge canvas painted in 1609, and again, it had a mesmerising effect on a fourteen year old. Samson slumps across Deliliah's lap, her pert breasts are exposed though she's fully dressed; clearly sex was on both their minds. A Philistine is cutting Samson's hair, his source of strength, while the whole dramatic scene is lit by a flaming brazier and a candle held by an ancient Philistine procuress. The oriental rug and the rumpled clothing of both Delilah and Samson are painted in sumptuous, technicolour detail.

Last, but by no means least in the inventory of my memory, is Paul Delaroche's painting of the execution of Lady Jane Grey, painted in 1833. And by a Frenchman! Absolutely riveting. It made my flesh creep and the hair on the nape of my neck prickle. The executioner, in his russet tights, waits with his axe to the right of the picture while the blindfolded Lady Jane is being assisted to the block. Her pale fingers stretch out in front of her as she kneels, while weeping attendants turn away from the bloody scene that is about to take place. The texture of her dress, in white satin, is so real you could crumple it in your fingers.

Not everybody likes this painting. Mr. Smart thought it a little contrived and slick. I loved it.

Bill Marsden thought it was "fan-fucking-tastic". Now there's pretty.

On he way back to Fulham, I kept looking at the buildings and the buses and the tube station at South Kensington with its brick-coloured ceramic tiles because Mr. Smart said art was everywhere.

Everywhere.

But nowhere so vivid, so stark, so deeply etched as it was in my adolescent mind in 1949.

Thank you, Mr. Smart.

And God bless the genius of Rubens, Bronzino and Delaroche.

And, oh yes, after Bronzino, copies of *Razzle* and *Health & Efficiency* seemed about as stimulating as my Aunty Dolly's knitted cardigans.

Street Parties

In a small, narrow street of terraced Victorian houses, trestle tables have been set out and covered with white bedsheets and Union Jacks. Bunting has been slung from one side of the street to the other and balloons fastened to the iron lampposts.

Men in collarless shirts and braces are carrying boxes out of the houses and from the open doors, a variety of cooking smells float and linger on the morning air. Women in headscarves and aprons occasionally appear in the doorways, some have flour on their arms up to the elbow. Others have emerged from the back of the terraces to snatch a few puffs of a Woodbine or "Player's Weights".

A scattering of small children are playing a curious version of street soccer, dodging and swerving past the men in shirtsleeves and kicking a soggy, half-deflated leather football. Occasionally a child collides with an adult and is delivered a rebuke — mostly verbal, but occasionally physical.

Three dogs, all terriers, bark excitedly and take it in turns to cock their legs against a lamppost.

It is a fine day, but a few clouds are scudding over the sun, sending long shadows along the street. At its far end, a cul-de-sac, two girls in floral print dresses are trying to prop up a huge poster of King George VI, but gusts of wind keep thwarting their efforts.

A man with tattooed forearms and the muscular build of a navvy goes to their rescue and His Majesty's image is fixed to a brick wall with masonry pins and a few hefty taps with a hammer.

A distant clock strikes eleven and one of the other men in shirtsleeves consults a fob watch taken from his vest pocket.

Women start to appear from the houses on both sides of the street carrying utensils, knives, forks, spoons, plates and mugs of a bewildering variety of shapes and colours. There doesn't appear to be a completely matching set of anything.

A gangling youth in boots and a green apron cycles into the street on a bike with a huge basket in front of the handlebars. In the basket is a cardboard box from which sprout a multitude of crackers, paper hats, streamers and little Union Jacks on sticks.

From the open doorways, men emerge carrying chairs. Dozens of them. Splay-backed kitchen chairs, rusty metal chairs with unsteady legs, bedroom chairs covered in faded chintz, babies' high chairs, stools, benches, planks of wood, cushions and blankets.

Time is moving on. The women smoking cigarettes have withdrawn into the houses and the smell of cooking food grows more pungent.

Two large men wearing fawn overalls are carrying a crate of beer from one of the houses — many more will follow.

44

At the cul-de-sac's end, a gramophone has been set up on a low, deal table. It has a large horn-speaker attachment. Next to it, a pile of black records have been stacked.

An elderly man, scrawny neck poking out from his collarless shirt, is winding up the gramophone. He is the music master for the day and has already placed his first black disc on the turntable. It will either be Elgar's "Pomp and Circumstance"; the national anthem or "Roll out the Barrel" — this is a given — they are the three most-played records on occasions such as this.

The clouds have passed and the little street is bathed in sunlight.

Within an hour, the trestle tables will be piled with food, pies, chips, jellies, jugs of custard, bowls of winkles, cockles, jam sandwiches, buns, sad little cakes made without fruit or butter.

The music master will start the gramophone turntable spinning, his old eyes watery with emotion and, as the men and women and children put on their paper hats and take their seats at the trestle tables, the slightly tinny sound of Elgar's "Pomp and Circumstance" bounces unevenly along the street.

It is August 1945. And just one of many streets in Fulham is about to celebrate VE Day with passion and laughter and singing that will continue on well into the night.

Street parties were a regular feature of Fulham life in the 1940s and 1950s, but they fell into three distinct categories. There was the single family affair, usually in summer, where furniture from a single house was moved into the street to accommodate visiting relatives who couldn't all be fitted inside. Then there was the neighbourhood celebration party, a birthday or anniversary where people would stand around in groups, the older ones perched on chairs, and drink brown ale or gin and orange or lemonade. They were the closest the Fulham working class got to having a cocktail party.

Then the big affairs, like VE Day, already described, or other occasions of great moment such as Fulham FC's promotion from second to first division, or the return of a soldier, sailor or airman from wartime duties.

Not every street in Fulham gave street parties. A curious, unspoken rule was that only the poorest streets gave parties. And splendid, uninhibited, deeply patriotic affairs they were too.

Even in a solidly working-class borough like Fulham, there were subtle differences between the labouring class, the workmen in collarless shirts and hobnailed boots and the so called "respectable" working class, the foremen, the bus inspectors, the clerks at the council offices.

These divisions were trivial and sometimes hard to detect but whether you had a street party or not, established your place in the pecking order.

In Hestercombe Avenue which was home to such luminaries as a police sergeant, a hairdresser from Whites Club in Piccadilly, a gas board official, an insurance salesman and a woman who gave piano lessons, there were never any street parties.

Or none that I can remember at least.

Fortunately I had enough friends scattered throughout the borough to ensure that I was invited to theirs.

And just where did the very best of these wonderful events take place? My all time favourites were Kilmaine Road, Sherbrooke Road and the Lewis Trust Buildings at Walham Green — all of them microcosms of vigorous, bawdy, comradely, working-class Fulham life.

I don't think they are quite so popular today.

But I could be wrong.

I do hope so.

Raised Seams

In a tiny, sloping street called Colehill Lane that led down onto the bustle of Fulham Palace Road, lived, in 1946, a Jew with no name.

Of course he did have a name, but as nobody from our family or circle of friends had ever spoken to him; he was to us, quite nameless.

I observed him with the guileless intensity of an eleven year old, magnetised by his oddness, his silent, withdrawn obscurity.

This much we knew. He was a bachelor. Perhaps 40 years old, perhaps 50. He wore curiously old-fashioned clothes, mostly black with wide lapels and tight, dandyish trousers with raised seams. He lived alone in a gloomy block of 1930s flats in Colehill Lane. His appearance invited gentle ridicule; the pale, narrow face with deep set, dark ringed eyes, the shock of raven black curls that would have shied away from the shadow of a comb.

He walked with a curious loping gait, long skinny legs encased in the black trousers with the raised seams.

He was a tailor, or to be more precise he "took work in" at his flat in Colehill Lane and did something called, mysteriously, "finishing". Presumably this meant other, mainstream tailors sending him garments to complete.

Perhaps his speciality was the creation of raised seams or double pleated turn-ups. Part of his fascination was that we never knew for sure what his "finishing" actually entailed.

I often saw him walking in Colehill Lane towards the Fulham Palace Road, head down, hands thrust deeply in his pockets, a look of blank concentration on his waxy face These excursions seemed pointless as he never entered a shop or was seen in possession of a bag or paper carrier.

Nobody we knew had ever spoken with him. Once a friend and I threw out a cheeky "hello" as we passed him on one of his solitary errands; all we could extract from him was a vapid stare and the merest grunt of acknowledgement.

What did he do for all those bleak years in his tiny flat in Colehill Lane? Well he "finished" other tailor's garments it is fair to assume. Did he sit cross-legged on a low table, a length of thread between his teeth, his needle arm moving in a tireless blur?

Did he cut swathes of tweed with oversized scissors against a paper pattern?

Did he sip tea while he worked, or something stronger.

Was he an only son, a survivor of the holocaust?

Did he weep or laugh or masturbate alone in his flat festooned with bolts of cloth, half-completed pantaloons, waistcoats, rolls of silk and wooden cotton reels?

Did he look up from his work and wonder why fate had dealt him such a hand?

Solitary. Silent. Isolated. A miniature world within a world. Had he ever been kissed, or been in love?

Had he ever laughed out loud, or screamed in anger and frustration?

What was the point of it all — his whole life — his stoic loneliness?

These were the unanswered questions that we all asked about the lonely Jew in Colehill Lane. Even my mother, ever the saviour of lame ducks, the befriender of homesick Chinamen and Indian students, failed to penetrate his carapace of isolation. Several attempts to engage him in small talk, the weather, the unpunctual nature of the trolley buses, all fell flat in the face of his unyielding silence.

Many years later, when I was serving in the British Army in Austria, my mother wrote to me and in the midst of the chatty gossip about home life, she mentioned the fact that the Jew without a name, had died. "Natural causes" according to the local *Fulham Chronicle*, but his body had lain undiscovered for a week until an official of the local gas board had alerted the police because he couldn't gain entry to the flat to read the meter.

The dead man was Polish, originally from Warsaw. He had been a survivor of the holocaust and not a single blood relative existed to claim his body. He was seventy-two.

And his name? Now here's the curious thing. In the *Fulham Chronicle* report, according to my mother, they said it was Grosch which didn't sound Polish, but in the next sentence, they spelled it Gross.

So even in death we didn't know his real name. He was the saddest man in all the world. I am still haunted by his memory, and he died 52 years ago.

First Kiss

I can't quite remember when I first decided to kiss Patricia. I know I was about thirteen years of age and I'd watched her for weeks, usually in Bishop's Park by the River Thames in Fulham.

She was older. Fifteen. She had a triangular, pretty face and pink rosebud lips even though she didn't wear lipstick. She laughed a lot, and the movement of her head as she did so made her curls dance. I particularly liked her eyes. They were so blue. They reminded me of my mother's china teapot she took out on special occasions, like when Indian students in turbans called on a Sunday for cucumber sandwiches and conversations with my father, the policeman. They were engineering students, these Indians, and they were a long way from home. My mother wanted to show them English hospitality. This involved cucumber sandwiches with the crusts cut off and blue china teapots.

Anyway, Patricia's eyes were as blue as Mum's teapot and no mistake. In Bishop's Park, on a Saturday, there was always a small dance band in the old Victorian bandstand, provided it wasn't raining.

Boys of sixteen would drift into the park in long draped jackets and shoes with inch-thick rubber soles called "brothel creepers". Their hair was miraculously long and swept round the back of their heads in ducks tails — or arses — as we used to say. I first saw Patricia with a group of these lads on Saturday night. She had a red coat which was probably her mother's or older sister's, if she had one — I never found out.

It was too big, this red coat, but even its bigness couldn't disguise the fact that Patricia had very well — formed breasts for a fifteen year old. She was quite short - today she might even be described as dumpy.

I decided I liked her a lot. She also had extremely slim ankles and well-shaped calves.

I had read in one of Hank Jansen's novels that this was a clear indicator of a passionate nature. That and of course a lower lip that hung open slightly revealing white teeth.

It took six Saturdays before I could get close enough to her to talk. Then with a surprising show of uncharacteristic courage, I asked her if she would come with me over Putney Bridge to the other side of the river. A new Black and White milk bar had opened and it was my intention to buy her a strawberry milkshake. The sophistication of a thirteen year old in 1948 was awesome.

And then, within another week, there we were walking side by side over Putney Bridge on a Saturday afternoon, about 4.30 by the big church tower on the Fulham side of the river.

She didn't say much as we walked, but just trailed her woollen gloved hand along the parapet of the bridge. There was a cool wind from the river even for a July day and it made her cheeks turn pink. She smelled good. Soap. And I think powder. Not much. Just a touch.

A barge drifted under the bridge carrying timber. Two seagulls, or maybe they were white pigeons, flapped past and then alighted on the parapet. One of them had a foot missing.

A bus passed, a number 14 bound for Putney Heath. It had come from the West End, Piccadilly, Hyde Park, Knightsbridge, Fulham Road, Fulham Palace Road, on its way to what I used to think was real country. Putney. The Green Man Pub.

Two boys on bikes sped by. They were both on bikes with drop handlebars. I hadn't yet progressed to drop handlebars: too dangerous, Mum said. It made you lower your head while you cycled and your vision of what lay ahead was dangerously restricted.

I knew one of the boys on the bikes. He was called Sid and had a face smothered in acne, with great pustules and lesions pitting his cheeks. He was the one who lent me Hank Jansen books which I had to hide from my mother because they were very rude.

They were usually about American men who smoked a lot and talked out of the corner of their mouths and when they kissed girls, the girls got very excited and gasped a great deal.

And then they did things, these girls. Willingly. It mostly involved letting these men touch their breasts and that bit of soft flesh above the stocking top. I'd never seen one of course, but Hank Jansen said they were very silky. The legs that is. And I suppose the stocking top as well. Another thing Hank Jansen said was that when you kissed a girl, really kissed her, with a film star kiss on the lips and you touched her breast at the same time she would melt into your arms. That's what he said. Melt into your arms. And not only that, you — the kisser — would experience an electric jolt of lust that would make your senses reel.

Just imagine. A girl melting into your arms and you experiencing an electrical jolt of lust that would make your senses reel!

Sid said he'd done it with a girl called Rita at the Lewis Trust Buildings in Fulham, but I didn't believe him. Even Rita, who had teeth missing, wouldn't have wanted to kiss poor Sid with his boils and scabs. But he did have a lot of Hank Jansen books. They were paperback and on their covers there was always a girl with her dress falling off, you could only see part of her breasts, but they stuck out like artillery shells and her legs were always visible right up to the top of the stocking.

Sid used to take the covers off the books before he lent them to me because he wanted to look at them when he was in bed at night. He used to illuminate them with a torch under his bedclothes and then hide them under the mattress in the morning.

So Patricia and I arrived on the Putney side of the bridge and crossed the road to the Black and White milk bar. It was next to the White Hart pub and a few workmen were standing around with beer on the pavement.

The milk bar was full of people sitting on round stools that were screwed to the floor. Waitresses in white coats and hats in the shape of shells were serving.

I bought two milkshakes in big glasses and gave one to Patricia. She put the straw in her mouth and sipped daintily. I wanted to kiss her right there, in the milk bar in front of the girls in hats shaped like shells and the other customers, many of whom were older men, about eighteen or nineteen years old. They wore gabardine slacks and were all smoking untipped cigarettes.

But I didn't kiss her. I stood as close as I could while we drank our milkshakes and smelled her powder and her soap.

She finished her drink and took out a tiny handkerchief to wipe her mouth. Her tongue was very pink and her teeth very white. Some strawberry milkshake had splashed onto her big red coat which was a silly thing to be wearing in July, I thought.

She didn't wipe the splashes off, she just left them there, proving that it was probably not her coat after all. If it had been hers, she would have wiped the splashes up immediately.

After we had finished, we walked back towards the bridge. "Do you like the bandstand?" I asked suddenly. It was the first time either of us had spoken since starting out from the Putney side of the bridge.

"It's alright," she said.

"You go there every Saturday, don't you?" I persisted.

She shrugged. "Sometimes," she said.

"We could dance there," I said, growing more reckless by the minute.

"You can't dance," she said flatly, running her gloved hand along the parapet.

"No," I said, deflated.

Halfway across the bridge, she stopped and looked down at the river. Three swans were wading in the mud of the towpath. A tiny gust of wind ruffled her hair and I saw the back of her white neck.

"Can I see you again?" I blurted out.

She stayed looking down at the swans, hardly moving at all.

"If you want," she said.

This was as good a signal as I was likely to get that day so I touched her shoulder and she turned around. Then I kissed her on the mouth and put my hand over her breast outside the thick red overcoat that didn't belong to her. I waited for her to melt into my arms and for me to experience an electric jolt of lust that would make my senses reel. Nothing.

She tasted of strawberry milkshake and smelled of powder and soap.

After about twenty seconds she pulled away, gently. My heart was pounding like a blacksmith's hammer and I felt good.

But no electric jolt.

"Let's go to the bandstand," she said, and as she spoke I could hear, faintly in the distance, the sound of a band playing "Jezebel", a Frankie Laine song I used to mime to at a friend's flat in the Lewis Trust Buildings on a Saturday evening. As we walked away, I felt a little twinge of emotion, not an electric jolt by any means, but something.

So this was what it was all about. This sex thing. Good. But not terrific.

I think Hank Jansen exaggerated a bit.

She had soft lips though, did Patricia.

I'll never forget that first kiss — it was absolutely wonderful.

Corpse

Brian was a small boy, pale-skinned and delicate. He lived in Burnfoot Avenue with his mother who, rumour had it, smothered him with love. His father had long ago flown the nest, leaving Brian and his mother to fend for themselves. She worked mornings in the hardware shop in Fulham Road because she knew the owner. She stood behind the long, polished deal counter wearing a green dust coat with pencils in the breast pocket and sold a cornucopia of items from 9 till 12 noon.

She only worked mornings when Brian was at school. During the school holidays, her mother, Brian's granny, came to stay, travelling by trolley bus from Hammersmith to look after Brian while mother did her bit in the hardware store. Granny was very old. At least 150, Brian said. But she was kind and spoiled him every bit as much as his mother.

One day in late autumn, I was cycling to Bishop's Park — it must have been a Saturday — when I saw Brian, his pale head lowered, kicking leaves along the gutter in Bishop's Park Road. He looked up when I drew level and I could see he'd been crying.

"My gran died this morning," he said. "She's going to be buried Tuesday."

I forget how I responded to this grim intelligence; at ten years old, my social skills were still in a state of hibernation.

Brian sighed like an old man, then looked straight at me. "Do you want to see her?" he said. "She's in the front room on the couch. The coffin don't come till Monday."

I wasn't sure if I really wanted to see his dead gran on a couch in their front room in Burnfoot Avenue, but I liked Brian. He seemed keen that I should.

"She looks alright," he said, "no blood nor nothing. Do you want to?"

I must have murmured assent because he immediately slung his leg over my crossbar and assumed the role of passenger. We cycled back to Burnfoot Avenue, about half a mile or so, and it was hard pedalling with Brian on the cross bar, his pale legs in grey shorts dangling either side of the bike.

When we arrived at his house, a small terraced villa with a stained glass St. George and the Dragon over the front door, Brian poked his hand into the letter box and pulled out a length of string on the end of which was a door key. This was a common practice in our neck of the woods; we had the same arrangement in Hestercombe Avenue.

"Mum's out," he said as he opened the door, "at the shop."

The hallway was dark and smelled of Mansion polish. A length of shiny blue lino covered the floor and the walls had lots of prints of country scenes, bridges over streams, hay ricks, churchyards, farm animals.

60

Brian switched on the light and a vapid orange glow illuminated the hall. "She's in here," he said and pushed open the door on the right to the front room. The room was small and square with a dark coloured carpet and drawn curtains. The only other piece of furniture in the room was a long couch. On it lay Granny, covered up to her chin with a navy blue blanket. Her head rested on a cushion with a tiny tassel and at first I thought her eyes were open, but they weren't.

Brian went up close and whispered, "Come and look."

I felt odd. Half repelled, but at the same time fascinated. The old woman's face looked waxy, the skin as white as a candle, but there was a blob of rouge on each of her cheeks. The hair, iron-gray and straggly, had been tied back with a piece of dark blue ribbon.

Brian turned to me. His face almost transparent in the faint light. "Do you want to touch her?" he said. "She's cold."

I shook my head. The thought alone terrified me.

We quit the room a minute or so later and Brian closed the door. "Don't tell nobody I let you see her," he said.

I said I wouldn't, then we cycled back to the park with Brian on the cross bar, in total silence. When we reached the park gates, Brian climbed off my bike and after chaining it to the railings, we went into the bandstand area, a wide expanse of asphalt surrounded by tall plane trees.

Brian looked at me again, big pale eyes shining. "She's a corpse," he said.

I'd never heard the word before and it impressed me. It sounded so final.

A corpse.

"Yes," I said, nonchalantly, "I know."

Many years later, I read that Brian had been charged with gross indecency in the Putney Bridge gents' toilet, caught, apparently, in what today would be described as "a position of unusual friendliness with a male person".

Granny was buried in the Fulham Cemetery close to the River Thames.

On Hallowed Ground

We once broke into the grounds of the Bishop of London's palace which lay behind high walls very close to the bustle of Fulham Palace Road.

It was surrounded by thick-trunked trees, heavy with shiny leaves and ripe acorns, an oasis of mock-rural calm in the middle of London. Its situation in such an area made it, to us, a place of mystery and challenge. Its main entrance was alongside municipal Bishop's Park, our regular playground, and a forbidding entrance it was too — tall iron gates between stone pillars and a small lodge covered in ivy.

Although it is 56 years since I last clapped eyes on the place, I do recall an image of a brooding mansion, surrounded by a gravel drive, with mullioned windows and sunshine glancing off the leaded-light panes.

Our purpose in penetrating this holy place was simple curiosity. No thought of personal gain, theft of altar artefacts or lead flashing from the roof entered our minds.

Actually that's not true. It entered our minds, but naked fear ensured that the thought was never translated into the deed.

There were three of us, I remember: myself, a girl called Suzie, (something of a tomboy) and a Spanish boy called August. We were all thirteen.

Having found footholds in a section of the massive ecclesiastical ramparts, it was simple manoeuvre to climb up and drop into the spacious grounds.

Having read Enid Blyton extensively since the age of ten, I remembered that when the Famous Five broke into private property on some morally defensible pretext, they always had to deal with packs of large dogs, Dobermann pinschers or Alsatians, and they pacified the foaming beasts by feeding them ham sandwiches. We three, I was quick to conclude, didn't have as much as a jam sandwich between us. Fortunately, no Baskerville hounds with yellowing teeth sprang from the undergrowth to rip into our unprotected bodies and we were able to circumnavigate the palace unharmed.

Today, I am certain, uniformed security guards with mobile phones and fierce cropped haircuts roam the grounds, as even bishops, perhaps bishops in particular, are targets for unhinged nutters of all stripes. In 1948, it was different. You could even leave your front door propped open in summer and burglary in Fulham was a rare event.

We stood and looked up at the grey granite edifice of the palace, but of life there was no sign. August, the Spanish boy, a Catholic, gazed at the windows with particular intensity. "He's not as important as the Pope," he said.

Suzie made a wry face. "And the Pope's not as important as God," she said in a voice of prim satisfaction.

I at once introduced a secular note into this erudite conversation and announced that my father, who was a policeman, could *arrest* the Bishop of London if he chose.

Not surprisingly, this remark baffled my two companions and I was obliged to explain that my utterance was the result of lateral thinking, although that is not how I put it to them.

"Look," I said, in the weary tones of a sophisticate, "my dad said that if anybody does wrong, duke or dustman, they go inside!"

More baffled looks from Suzie and August.

"What's he done wrong?" asked August.

"Who?" said Suzie.

"The bishop," said August.

"Nothing," said Suzie.

"Then why does your dad want to arrest him?" said August to me.

"He doesn't," I said, a sense of panic creeping over me. "I never said he did."

"You did," said Suzie.

"Duke or dustman," said August.

"Yes, but if the bishop did something wrong, my dad would arrest him," I said.

"How would he know?" said August.

"How would he know what?" said Suzie.

"That the bishop had done something wrong," said August.

At this stage, I recall the conversation slowly filtering into silence, the questions we had raised were too awesome to contemplate further. Besides which, I was certain they thought I was simply showing off because my dad was a policemen.

August then suggested we knock on the front door of the palace and ask if we could do "a bob-a-job". He was a Spaniard of course and his understanding of the Boy Scout tradition was a trifle hazy.

We decided that knocking on the massive, studded door was not, after all, a good idea. Instead we drifted around the building past piles of compost and abandoned wheelbarrows and long rakes leaning up against the ivy-covered walls.

A blackbird, the largest I'd ever seen, scurried across the gravel path and then took off, flying in a low arc to alight on an overhanging branch. It looked extraordinarily evil, this bird, as it sat on the branch and surveyed us with its unblinking yellow eyes.

At the far side of the palace was an extensive area of lawn where, I learnt years later, the bishop's garden parties were held. The lawn was a little unkempt and studded with daisies, and Suzie stooped and picked a few.

It was then, at that precise moment, that I realised that Suzie was not just a friend, or a girl, she was a *female*.

I think it was the delicate way she plucked the little daisies from the lawn and the way in which she carefully formed them into a chain, something I'd never witnessed before. When she put the daisy chain, complete, onto her tousled head, I felt a mysterious surge of emotion. It wasn't pubescent sexuality or anything like that, more of a revelation, a falling away of scales from the eyes.

This grubby creature, thirteen years old, in a frock and sandals, was so *different*. It is quite impossible to describe how intense this feeling was with any degree of accuracy, but intense it most certainly was.

August didn't seemed to have noticed and we just continued our walk around the palace grounds. Of another human being, we saw not a sign.

Later, in Bishop's Park, next to the palace, I found a threepenny bit in my pocket and bought an ice-cream cone from Maria, the Italian lady who kept a barrow outside the park gates. All three of us shared the ice cream, even Suzie with the crown of daisies sitting, oh so lightly, on her auburn curls.

The site of the Bishop of London's Palace was once surrounded by the largest moat in England. It was over a mile long until 1920 when demands for land to extend the Fulham Palace Road made it necessary to fill the moat in.

The old palace, with its magnificent red brick Tudor courtyard, was the official home of the Bishops of London from AD704 until 1973. The gardens were famous in earlier centuries, running down close to the River Thames with their wisteria walk, great oak and medieval knot garden.

Vines were planted very early on and the grapes produced attracted favourable comment from many quarters of the kingdom. Bishop Grindal sent Queen Elizabeth I a gift of grapes which, legend has it, she described as being among the plumpest she had ever tasted.

The palace grounds are now open to the public and there is no need to risk life and limb by climbing over the walls; the palace itself is a museum. Walking around the grounds in 2002, it is remarkable how rural it feels. The great trees and sweeping lawns still remain and, even with the nearby hiss of traffic on Putney Bridge, you could half imagine yourself in the heart of the countryside.

A Gentleman Amateur

The cafe at Walham Green is situated close to the underground station and, as the tube trains rattle past, the mugs and plates and steel cutlery clatter in sympathy on the blue Formica tables. Whorls of cigarette smoke hang in the air like wreaths, mixing with the fierce smell of hot fat and frying onions.

The cafe is full of large men in work clothes, overalls, heavy boots, leather waistcoats. In front of each man is a plate piled high with food. There are chips on every plate, some with fried eggs and bacon, others with mounds of minced meat, onions, cabbage and bright green peas that have been mashed into a puree. Some of the men are holding mugs of tea in their enormous fists and forking down the food with their free hand. A few are smoking and eating at the same time.

A pyramid of food is transferred into an open mouth, chewed but twice, and then swallowed. Up comes an untipped Player's Weight, drawn on hard and returned to the edge of the table where it sits in a brown groove left by a previous smoker. Even before a lungful of smoke is exhaled, more food is shovelled in and two small boys sitting by the window watch in fascination as big, muscular men chew mouthfuls of thick bacon and blow smoke from their nostrils at the same time.

69

Most of the men are labourers employed directly by the Fulham Borough Council and they are engaged on a major project in the Fulham Road which involves digging up the pavements and pouring cement into holes big enough to hide a bus.

Earlier, just outside the cafe, the two boys had watched as one of the men, built like Atlas with forearms as big as a sprinter's thighs, operated a pneumatic drill to pierce the two-inch-thick tarmac in the road.

The noise was terrific and the man had to lean heavily on the drill to stop it bouncing haphazardly over the surface. This man is a demi-god. Over six feet tall with shoulders so wide he has to turn sideways to come through the cafe doorway. His hands, now gripping a pint of hot tea, are like hams with knuckles the size of walnuts. In his spare time, he lifts weights at the St. George's Bodybuilding Club in Putney. He is a hero to the two boys who sit quietly by the window sipping mugs of tea.

He eats his food with slow deliberation, loading each forkful with chips, bacon and a dollop of the squashed peas. When he chews, the muscles around his jawbone clench and unclench with a steady rhythm. He takes a draught of hot tea to wash down the food and then a big drag at his cigarette before he puts it down on the table.

Then it's back to the food, his hands moving in a steady, hypnotic arabesque as he tackles the mountain of steaming nourishment in front of him.

The boys can't take their eyes off him as he eats and smokes and drinks.

He wears metal-tipped boots, size twelve, and they are covered in cement dust. When his plate is clear, he pushes it across the table and sits back, stretching. His chest must be 50 inches in circumference, at least.

The cafe owner, a tiny man with a fringe of hair around his shiny bald pate, hurries across and puts another plate in front of the man. On it, a hunk of apple pie sits in a lake of vivid yellow custard like a stricken ocean liner. The man picks up his spoon and plunges it into the pie, then raises it, dripping, to his mouth. In four mouthfuls it is gone. So is the custard. He finishes his tea in a single gulp and then crushes his cigarette out in the empty dish.

The cafe owner has forgotten to put out the ashtrays. He is a little overawed by the big man with the broad back, his donkey jacket stretched almost to bursting over those massively developed latissimus dorsi. The jacket has the words FULHAM COUNCIL stencilled over the back, but the letters are faded and cracking. The two boys watch as the big man stands up, unfolding his enormous form to its full height, probably six foot six. At least. Maybe more.

As he turns to go, one of the boys, a gawky fifteen year old, stands up and then moves towards him. He holds a book in one hand and a pencil in the other. As the giant moves towards the door, the boy holds out the open book. It's a magazine with glossy paper. On the open page is a black and white photograph of a man in a white vest standing on a platform. At his feet is a huge barbell loaded at each end with metal plates. The man in the photograph is poised as if about to pounce, his gigantic arms outstretched downwards, his thighs like columns of grooved marble.

"Can I have your autograph," the boy says, almost apologetically.

The giant takes the book, and the pencil and scribbles quickly across the photograph. What he writes looks like "Dave". It is enough.

The boy takes back the book as if handling a religious icon and says, "Thanks". Dave smiles and swings away towards the door. The small boy is red with excitement and he goes back to his friend at the window table. Dave goes outside and moves out of their sightline.

The cafe now seems half-empty. The cafe owner comes across to clear Dave's table and picks up the few coins Dave has left there. He turns towards the counter, balancing the plates and dish and then addresses the whole cafe. "Dave might make the British team," he says. "*Health & Strength* reckon he's one of our best lifters."

The two boys know this. The magazine that Dave has autographed is the self-same *Health & Strength*. The photograph was of Dave — David Dunning, then 22 years old, but at the age of eighteen already capable of a 400lb dead lift and a 300lb bench press.

The *Health & Strength* magazine solemnly forecast that he could make the British Olympic weightlifting team if he could improve just one of the three Olympic "lifts". This lift, curiously known as the "snatch" is one that required the athlete to raise the loaded barbell above his head from the ground in one unbroken movement. It is a spectacular lift that calls for speed and co-ordination. Being tall, Dave has to make the barbell travel a lot further than his squat, bulkier competitors to get it to "locked-out" arms' length.

The other two lifts in the Olympic trio are "the press" and the "clean and jerk".

Will Dave be able to improve his snatch in time to make the Olympic team?

Who knows? The two boys in the window of the cafe talk excitedly about the technicalities of weightlifting. "Dave splits when he snatches," says one. "Better if he squatted. More push from his legs."

The gawky boy nods. "But tall blokes usually split. It's those little lifters like that Mohammed Nasr from Egypt who squat. He's got 30 inch thighs."

"Wow," says the other, and they both take a draught of refreshing tea.

Outside, Big Dave has returned to work, his big spatulate hands wielding a shovel as if it were a teaspoon. He labours heavily, relentlessly digging, lifting, pushing barrows of cement, manhandling thick paving stones into position. He's removed his donkey jacket and works stripped to the waist. Muscles gleaming and rippling under his pale skin.

That evening, after eight and a half hours, of heavy physical labour, he will go home to his flat in Kilmaine Road and wash himself at the sink in the tiny kitchen. His wife, a small, pretty woman prematurely lined and greying, will make a corned beef sandwich for him and pour out a pint of full cream milk.

After this modest — for Dave — repast, he will change into a baggy tracksuit and plimsoles and catch a number 14 bus to Putney. There, at the St. George's Club above the Duke's Head pub, he will train with heavy weights for two hours. Lifting, squatting, curling, pressing.

During a brief break in this punishing routine, he will drink another pint of milk and eat a bar of chocolate.

At ten o'clock, training done, he will catch the bus home, wash at the sink again, and go to bed. Dave is an Olympic hopeful. He wants to make the British team.

Here is a man who works as a labourer six days a week performing feats of strength and endurance and trains four times a week lifting enormous poundages and practising his squats and splits and presses and jerks. He is the personification of the true amateur, a living example of the Olympic spirit. Fulham will be so proud if Dave makes the British team.

His counterparts in America and Russia and Poland and Bulgaria, all Olympic hopefuls, have been "adopted" by the state. Not for them the need to labour eight hours a day in order to put bread on the table at home. One of the Americans has even been given a place at university, his subject, physical education or something vaguely related to it.

Those who make it to their country's Olympic team will be at a peak of strength and fitness that can only be achieved by dedicating themselves full time to their sport.

A few weeks later, the British Olympic weightlifting team is announced.

Dave Dunning is not among them.

Health & Strength magazine runs an editorial extolling Dave's "sporting instinct" and wishing him better luck next time.

The gawky boy who obtained his autograph puts the magazine with Dave's photo and signature into a small suitcase under his bed. Better luck next time.

You Ain't Foolin' Me

The whiskey and cigarette soaked voice of Jimmy Witherspoon floated from the old gramophone as he delivered perhaps the greatest blues song ever written. His phrasing and articulation, so loaded with emotion and raw energy, made the three thirteen year olds in the small room sit transfixed as the music took possession, not just of their ears, but their bodies and their souls.

"You can fool all of the people, some of the time —
You can fool some of the people, all of the time —
But woman, you ain't foolin' me."

As one of the three young people in the room, it was my first real introduction to that superb art form, the American blues, sung, of course, by a black singer with more sense of passion and melody and truthfulness than all of the 1990s rap artists rolled into one.

Until then, most of the music that I had experienced had been the bland ballads of middle America and the ghastly rumpety-pumpety fake rhythms of the BBC's "light" orchestras.

I had also sat in the wings of the Sadlers Wells Theatre while my sister performed in the chorus of various operas. This was not an ideal way to introduce a stroppy youth to classical music.

Accompanied by my mother, I was there to escort my sister Mary home from to Fulham after the opera finished, a role which, as a thirteen year old, I found about as exhilarating as having my sinuses drained. I only ever heard the last ten minutes of any opera Mary was involved with and, you guessed it, most of them involved fat ladies singing while dying or occasionally dying while singing.

It was some years before I saw a full length opera, *Don Giovanni*, and I was ashamed that I had so foolishly condemned the genre in my callow youth, based on such a slight exposure to it.

However, back in 1948, in a tiny council flat near Walham Green, I did realise that after listening to Jimmy Witherspoon and Bessie Smith and Memphis Minnie and Blind Willie McTell, that I had discovered music I would love forever; and furthermore, music that would never be surpassed by any new forms that emerged over the remainder of the 20th century.

The proud owner of the stack of 78-inch vinyls in that tiny flat was a lad called Merton. I hardly knew him, but I had been taken there by another resident of the Lewis Trust Buildings, a gawky girl of thirteen, the unobtainable, the achingly untouchable June who, in spite of being taller than all the thirteen year olds we hung out with and as thin as a rake, was capable of reducing most thirteen year-old boys of her acquaintance to a quivering jelly of unrequited lust by the merest toss of her straw-coloured hair.

She had actually asked me to accompany her to Merton's flat because he had let it be known that his mum, a woman of rumbustious charms and a bosom to die for, had been "going out" with an American airman based in London and he had given Merton the collection of 78s, as a bribe no doubt, not to reveal his mum's association with the airman to his stepfather who was away in the north of England on some unspecified, but deeply secret work which involved absences of several months.

To be asked by June to go visiting Merton's flat to listen to jazz and blues records was a tremendous boost to my ego. For years, we had all assumed she was "Chalky's" girl. Chalky was another Lewis Trust Buildings resident who himself was given to musical evenings when his parents were at the pub, but his music, which I also liked, was the aforesaid Frankie Laine and the lung-bursting Stan Kenton.

Hearing blues for the first time was like losing your virginity while eating a cream doughnut and smoking an untipped Capstan full-strength. All one's senses were twanged into a state of foaming ecstasy. And at thirteen, believe me, I was a right little foamer.

Jimmy Witherspoon and the blues weren't the only thing to hit me between the eyes on that special day in a tiny flat in the Lewis Trust Buildings at Walham Green. There was the roller skating experience! Come on, we're talking 1948! Now I knew roller skates existed and I knew children in Fulham who actually roller skated.

Let's face it, we weren't entirely naive.

Not entirely.

But just a bit, maybe.

However, it was more than just a revelation when the unattainable June, yes the same straw-colour-haired goddess who had introduced me to Jimmy Witherspoon and the blues, suggested we all visit the Eel Brook Common near Parson's Green to witness a roller skating event, an event that had been signalled in the local paper as a "Fund Raising Festival of Fun" where an all-girl troupe from faraway Belgium would give a roller skating display in national costume. Can you imagine the unbridled excitement, anticipation and explosive lust that such an event would trigger in the imagination of a thirteen year old who had yet to leave the shores of dear England.

The actuality, of course, was not as earth-shattering as the advance publicity suggested. It did take place at Eel Brook Common, a patch of ill-kept municipal grass and cinder near Parson's Green, just off the New King's Road, and it was for charity, but just what charity is now a hazy mist and beyond recall.

What was rather special however, was the troupe of girls who skated in formation around the common in national Belgium costume. They were all very pretty. And young. And they wore the shortest skirts I'd ever seen.

Subsequent research into the national costumes of Europe have revealed that not even the wildest fantasist and drooling voluptuary could ever claim that any country in that great continent had a history of female roller skaters in tiny skirts and fluffy knickers. It is hard for anyone today, young or old, to fully appreciate the effect of such a spectacle on a thirteen year old who, up until that moment, had lived a somewhat sheltered life.

I cannot begin to do justice to the event. But I'll try. Imagine a dozen tall, willowy girls of about eighteen on metal roller skates gliding around Eel Brook Common in tiny skirts and lacy knickers, waving and smiling a the handful of spectators while three or four elderly Belgian women, not I hasten to add in knickers that could be observed of any sort whatsoever, held out collection tins!

Does all this sound ridiculous? Absurd even?

Of course it does.

But it happened. In Fulham. In 1948.

On the very same day I heard my first Jimmy Witherspoon record.

And they said the 1960s were a "swinging" decade.

Give me a break.

The 1940s were bloody fantastic. I know. I was there.

The Fault Lies Not Within Our Stars

Two thirteen-year-old boys are sitting on a wooden bench in Bishop's Park. One is skinny with fair hair cut short and a mild feathering of acne on his chin. The other is plump, red-faced and dark-eyed with a riot of black curls that cover the tops of his ears. The chubby one wears a wristwatch, a rarity among boys in 1948. The bony one holds a thick book on his lap and is reading aloud from it.

"How foolish your fears seem now Calpurnia." He speaks in a flat, typical London accent that is a grade or so above full-blooded cockney.

The other boy cranes over and looks at the book which the skinny one closes with a snap.

"I'm not doing bloody Calpurnia," says the chubby one.

"Caesar's wife," says the skinny boy.

"I know, but I'm not doing it. I mean *her*."

"Alright, do a bit of Cassius," says the skinny one.

"*You* do it."

"I will."

"Go on then."

The skinny boy stands up. He is quite tall for his age, 5 feet 10½ inches. He will never grow any bigger than this for the rest of his life. Except in circumference. "I was born as free as Caesar, so were you — we both have fed as well and both can endure the winter's cold as well as he, for once upon a raw and gusty day, the troubled Tiber chafing with her shores, Caesar said to me "Dearest thou Cassius, now leap with me into this angry flood and swim to yonder point?" Upon the word, accoutred as I was, I plunged in and bade him follow, so indeed he did — the torrent roared . . ."

The skinny boy pauses and runs a hand through his hair. "I'm not sure of the next bit. Some old bloke called Anchises or something."

The chubby boy grins. "I like that speech. I like that stuff about the foaming Tiber."

"Yeah," says the skinny boy, "but I don't know all of it."

"Now this man is become a God!" cries chubby suddenly. "And Cassius is a wretched creature and must bend his body if Caesar carelessly but nod on him."

"Blimey," says the skinny boy, admiringly, but takes up the challenge. "Why man he doth bestride the world like a colossus."

"The fault, dear Brutus, is not in our stars but in ourselves that we are underlings," cries chubby.

They both collapse on the park bench laughing helplessly.

After a few moments, their laughter subsides. The chubby boy blows his nose on a silk handkerchief. It is another clue, along with the wristwatch, that he comes from a well-to-do family. "I can do Shylock," he says.

"Yeah," says the skinny one. "Boas said you were as good as Sam Kelso."

"But Sam got the part," says chubby.

"Well he is older and Jewish," says the skinny boy.

"Well so am I."

"Yeah."

"And Sam's got red hair. Not many Jewish boys have red hair. He is a brilliant Shylock though."

The skinny boy shrugs. What does he know of such things? He's happy though; he's got the part of Salanio in *The Merchant of Venice*, the school play. His chubby friend, hasn't been cast. Pity. He has a fine voice.

"Do a bit of Shylock," the skinny boy says, sympathetically.

"I'm not doing it in a piss-taking accent," says the chubby boy shaking his black curls. "My dad says it's anti-Semitic to do it in a pisstaking accent."

"What do you mean?" says the skinny boy, scratching his ravaged chin. "What piss-taking?"

"Well you know, 'My life, already, my boy'."

The skinny boy looks blank.

Now the chubby boy adopts a grotesque mid-European accent. "Alright, already," he growls.

"Oh come on," says skinny, not really comprehending.

The chubby boy stands up on the bench and clears his throat portentously. "He hath disgraced me and hindered me half a million, laughed at my losses, mocked at my gains, scorned my nation, thwarted my bargains, cooled my friends, heated mine enemies — and what's his reason?"

Here the chubby boy pauses, his face serious, he seems to have aged ten years. He pushes a lock of hair from his forehead with the back of his hand. The skinny boy is seated, watching, his lips silently following the chubby boy's words.

"And what's his reason?" the chubby boy continues. "I am a Jew. Hath not a Jew eyes, hath not a Jew hands, organs, dimensions, senses, affections, passions? Fed with the same food, hurt with the same weapons, subject to the same diseases, healed by the same means, warmed and cooled by the same winter and summer as a Christian is? If you prick us do we not bleed? If you tickle us do we not laugh? If you poison us do we not die? And if you wrong us, shall we not revenge?"

The chubby boy has a remarkably deep baritone for a thirteen year old and it is a curiously moving rendition.

For a moment, both boys remain silent. They have both been seduced by the sheer, heart-stopping magic of Shakespeare's language spoken out loud. This is because they have been indoctrinated in its beauty by their headmaster, Guy Boas, a Shakespearian scholar and librarian at the famous Garrick Club.

It is curious, even amazing, that two lads in Fulham should be so enchanted by the compelling words of the bard. It is all down to Guy Boas. He had the rare ability to unlock the doors that so often bar young people from understanding and subsequently loving Shakespeare.

It is 1948. And a policeman's son and his friend, a Jewish boy whose father is a musician with a small jazz band, are both quoting great chunks of prose — from memory — in Fulham's municipal park by the River Thames.

An old man passes by with a big, ragged looking Alsatian. He has heard snatches of what the two boys are saying, but he merely glances in their direction.

"Bleeding crackers," he says, quite distinctly and his dog barks twice.

Lewis Trust Buildings

The three of us stood by the used car lot near Putney Bridge. It was just a patch of earth and flattened rubble, a bomb-site that had once been part of a parade of shops, before the doodle-bug had demolished it. Now it had a fence of galvanised wire surrounding it and beyond the fence were a dozen or so second-hand cars: two Austin Sevens with flat tyres, a 1939 Austin Goodwood saloon in rusting silver with dark blue leather upholstery (£108, including bald tyres). There were a few unrecognisable makes and one real beauty, a 1930 Buick with left-hand drive, a big bonnet with a huge chrome fender and a wide running board. Jet black with silver trim. "Chalky" White touched my arm. "Look at that," he said, "American. I want it."

So did I, but I kept silent. Chalky turned to June, a tall, blondish girl of about fourteen.

"I'm getting it," he said.

June laughed. She was taller than Chalky, by at least six inches. "It's £98," she said, "you haven't got any money."

"I have," he said, and pulled a ten shilling note from his pocket.

We laughed, June and I. Poor Chalky.

"What you do," said Chalky, "is pay a bit now and the rest over a few weeks."

More laughter.

"I got my paper round," Chalky insisted angrily.

"But you can't drive," said June.

"You can be a right cow sometimes," said Chalky.

"I'm cold," I said, "let's go."

We walked up the New Kings Road towards World's End, Chalky in a mac with a belt, me in a "T" shirt and grey trousers and June — the delectable, unobtainable June — in an angora sweater with a fuzz or fur that stood out like a halo when the sun was behind her. She was tall and thin, with very blue eyes. I wasn't quite sure whether she was Chalky's real girlfriend or not. We were all fourteen.

Chalky and June lived in the Lewis Trust Buildings at Walham Green in Fulham. They were built in 1922 to house the urban poor, a clutch of tall grey granite buildings with a central court area like a prison exercise yard. Chalky's parents were old. He'd been a late arrival. Father was a labourer for the Fulham Borough Council and when you saw him, at the tiny flat in the Lewis Trust Buildings, he always looked exhausted. A small, wiry man covered in cement dust, with big workman's boots.

Every Saturday, or almost every Saturday, Chalky would give his parents the proceeds from his paper round, a few shillings, and they would go to the Swan pub in Walham Green and drink mild and bitter and perhaps a gin and orange for chalky's mum if the money ran that far. Just occasionally Chalky's dad would open his own pay packet and take out half-a-crown to buy his wife a second gin and orange, but usually they made Chalky's paper round money last until closing time at 10.30 p.m.

We, meantime, Chalky, June, myself and a few other boys and girls would be in Chalky's parents flat playing Frankie Laine records and smoking Craven "A"s. Everybody, the lads that is, wanted to neck with June, but being a bit of a tomboy, she proclaimed such activity as "daft".

There was always a bottle of brown ale in Chalky's flat. We would pass it round, each taking a long swig and then wiping the neck of the bottle on our shirts or jumpers. June too, except when she wiped the bottle neck, she left angora fluff stuck to it.

I had to be home by 9.30 so I never stayed until Chalky's parents came back from The Swan.

June went into Chalky's bedroom one Saturday and they closed the door. I put on a Frankie Laine record, "Jezebel", and turned up the sound. "If ever the devil was born — without a pair of horns — Jezebel it was youuu!" When the record was finished, I put on another — Johnny Ray singing "Cry". "When your sweetheart sends a letter of goodbyeee, it's not secret, you'll feel better if you cryeeee." Even when Johnny Ray had finished, Chalky and June were still in the bedroom.

There was just me and Sid and Dennis and a girl from Hammersmith I didn't know, left in the little lounge. The girl was very fat and about sixteen. Older than the rest of us.

Dennis, who had a Tony Curtis haircut, tried to neck with her, but she whined about having a sore throat so he lit a Craven "A" and smoked it ostentatiously. Me and Sid tried to hear what was going on behind Chalky's bedroom door, but Dennis and the fat girl from Hammersmith who wouldn't kiss him kept putting records on the record player. Stan Kenton's, "Peanut Vendor". Lots of loud trumpet music.

Sid was picking at a particularly angry pustule on his cheek and sitting on the arm of the old sofa with the tartan cover. "Do you think they're doing it?" he asked.

Nobody knew for sure. We had our suspicions, but that was all.

Eventually, Chalky and June came out of his room and joined the four of us. June looked calm and as pretty as usual. Chalky had an embarrassed grin on his face. When he thought June wasn't looking, he made a gesture with his forefinger, injecting it into the balled fist of his other hand.

"I've got to go home," said Dennis, who lived in Chelsea. He was clearly angry and jealous because he had suffered a dual humiliation, the fat girl from Hammersmith with the sore throat had refused to kiss him, and June, who he loved more than life itself, as we all did, had spent at least ten minutes with Chalky in his bedroom.

When Dennis and Sid had left and June had gone to the toilet and the fat girl from Hammersmith was rummaging through Chalky's pitiful collection of records, Chalky took a Durex packet out of his pocket and then he winked.

June came out of the toilet and saw him. "Charlie!" she said, because that was his real name.

Chalky put the Durex packet back into his pocket and actually blushed.

"We didn't do nothing," said June, glaring at Chalky, "no matter what he says, we didn't do nothing."

I was pleased, not because I hated Chalky, but at least he hadn't done it with her.

I left at 9.15 and walked home along the Fulham Road. When I got to my parents' flat in Hestercombe Avenue, my mother was in the hall waiting. "Why did you go out without your jumper?" she asked. Little did she know that I had seen a packet of Durex and drunk brown ale and smoked two Craven "A" cigarettes and that Chalky had *not* done it with June in the bedroom at the Lewis Trust Buildings.

All in all, an evening of high drama and not a little satisfaction.

Hestercombe Avenue

The houses in Hestercombe Avenue were solid, three-storey jobs with small walled gardens at the rear and coal cellars. Today those cellars are filled with wine racks or converted into computer rooms for the dot-com executives and merchant bankers who now own them. When I lived there, virtually all the houses were divided into flats, for two and sometimes three families. The cellars weren't filled with racks of Chateau Lynch Bages, but piles of coal.

We lived at number 4 Hestercombe Avenue on the ground floor so we had the use of a tiny garden with a stunted pear tree and a scrap of lawn.

The other tenants in the house were Mr. and Mrs. Bailey. He was the park keeper at Bishop's Park and his wife, Kate, was, not to put too fine a point on it, slightly loopy. He wore a park keeper's uniform and walked to work in heavy boots carrying a stick with a metal point for picking up leaves. Kate used to talk to herself upstairs on the landing that separated the two flats and would occasionally yell out quotations from Shakespeare to nobody in particular. She was well read, for a park keeper's wife, was mad Kate.

Everybody rented property in those days as Fulham was soundly a working-class area and home owners, landlords and the like lived in Chelsea, which was another country.

Our landlord, Mr. Hopkins, lived in Anderson Street off the Kings Road in Chelsea and Mum had to catch a 22 bus down the Kings Road to pay the rent every week. Only occasionally would Hopkins, a wiry man with a pinched and lined face, come to visit us, driving a big Rover car with fat tyres.

The tenants in most of the houses in Hestercombe Avenue were what would be described as respectable working class. No labourers in cement-covered boots or garage mechanics in greasy overalls, but men who wore the uniform of postmen or meter-readers for the gas board or park keepers like Mr. Bailey or policemen like my father, although he was the only policeman in Hestercombe Avenue. When he cycled to work, he wore a mac over his uniform and didn't put his helmet on until he got to the station. This, my mum explained, was in order to maintain the tone of the neighbourhood.

Our next door neighbours on the right were Mr. and Mrs. Gear, an elderly couple. She had suffered a stroke in her 50 and was now a frail, shuffling figure in a woolly hat and shoes with little buttoned straps. Mr. Gear, pin-neat in a black coat and black trousers, always wore a Homburg hat and pearl-grey gloves. He looked remarkably up market for Hestercombe Avenue with his clipped moustache and polished shoes. He was the hairdresser at Whites Club in Piccadilly and he travelled to work each day on the 14 bus looking every inch the city gent. My father said, without a trace of malice, that Mr. Gear "aped" his superiors at the club, hence the dress code, and the accent which was faintly reminiscent of a retired Indian colonel.

Two doors further down lived another hairdresser, but he called himself a barber. This distinction was lost on me in 1950, but my parents knew exactly what it meant.

The barber's name was Jack Risk, a cheery, toothy cockney who worked in a barber's shop in the Munster Road. His wife, Gladys, died young from breast cancer and they had five daughters. For some reason, when talking about the Risk family, my father would say, "Jack Risk has five daughters, all girls!" This remark always reduced my mother to giggles which she suppressed behind a hanky. "Jack Risk has five daughters, all girls." I never thought it was remotely funny.

Nobody owned a car in Hestercombe Avenue and indeed none of the houses had garages when they were built between 1898 and 1903. Only on Saturdays, when Fulham Football Club were playing at home, did you see a car in the road: usually a Morris Minor or, more rarely, a Sunbeam Talbot.

Round the corner from Hestercombe was Dorncliffe Road: more Edwardian three storeys and a few bigger houses with steps leading up to the first floor.

At the far end of Dorncliffe lived my friend August Kratz with his Spanish family. They were "enduring modest circumstances", Mrs. Kratz said in her thick Spanish accent.

August had a sister, Carmen, a year younger than he. She was a dark-haired, pretty girl, but a birth defect had left her with one badly withered leg. Her good leg was shapely and she favoured it as she walked.

One day, I was in the Kratz's tiny flat at the top of the house in Dorncliffe, where they had two attic rooms, and August and I were swapping comics. My old *Beanos* for his *Dandys*, my *Wizards* for his *Champion*. As I riffled through his pile of dog-eared publications, I came across a slim photograph album. August pushed it to one side. "Carmen's leg book," he said, by way of explanation, I picked it up and opened it. It was full of pictures of girls legs. Just the legs. Glossy photos from American magazines of silk stocking advertisements. Pictures of girls in swimming costumes, but just from the waist down. Page after page or perfect calves and thighs.

Later, back at my own flat, I told my mother about Carmen's leg book and she went directly into the scullery without saying anything. I followed her and she was standing by the small sink and crying, silently.

Once, in 1949, my dad was offered the chance to buy 4 Hestercombe Avenue from the landlord, Mr. Hopkins. £800 freehold. He had the money, I think, in the Post Office. But he refused to buy it, didn't want "a millstone round his neck", he said. I still have the image of my father in his dark blue serge police trousers and a baggy woollen jumper standing at his makeshift bench in the cellar and telling me that he didn't want to buy the house.

The cellar, or that part of it that didn't contain coal, was my father's sanctuary, a little corner that was exclusively his, the place where he "pottered" as mother described it. He had no actual hobbies: no golf, no darts at the pub, no billiards. He read avidly, of course, but being a policeman, he wasn't by nature a "joiner". But he did potter and this pottering led him into demonstrating a quite remarkable creative skill in making things. He made a pirate galleon from bits of old firewood, its sails of painted cardboard. He rigged up a Heath-Robinson kind of electric motor from old fob-watch parts and torch batteries.

He created a wonderful doll's house from orange boxes with curtains at the tiny windows, chairs, tables, beds and rugs, all in miniature, in the four little rooms. He made me a set of plasticine animals based on the characters in Mary Tourtel's *Rupert Bear* stories; a wise old goat with a beard, horns and a shepherd's crook, Rupert himself, the ubiquitous bear, with his yellow check pants and black button eyes.

It was extraordinary to watch him, a big man with thick, strong fingers, working with a natural dexterity on tiny items, splinters of wood, scraps of linoleum, discarded clock springs, buttons, fragments of glass. As he worked on these fiddly little projects, you could see that it was also his thinking time. It was here, I learnt later, that he reviewed his life, his hopes and his fears. In the cellar, standing in his check slippers on the cold stone floor, silently, big hands operating with the delicacy of a surgeon as he pondered on what might have been, or why fate had dealt him the hand that it had.

He was not an unhappy man. He had a loving family and a secure job. But he was a disappointed man. He knew in his heart, down in some secret, hidden part of himself, that he could have soared to great heights. He was immensely well read, articulate, imaginative, but a little afraid of pushing too hard or reaching too high because above all, he feared rejection. If he didn't seek promotion or advancement, then there would be no rejection.

"Play it safe" was his motto, and yet being a policeman in London was not a soft option. It was a tough job. He had the intellectual resources to have become Commissioner of the Metropolitan Police, of this I am certain, but he lacked the will, the naked ambition and ruthlessness to actually scale that mountain.

Sometimes I would sit on the cellar steps and he would break off from whatever he was working on and, quite spontaneously, start telling me tales of his time in the trenches in the Great War, or of his early days at school. Once he got into his stride, we could be there for hours or until the tiny figure of my mother would appear at the top of the stairs with mugs of tea and biscuits. She knew this was an important time for both of us, what today would be pretentiously called "bonding".

They were good, these sessions.

Mind food. Brain nourishment.

There was no television to claim our attention and usurp these precious hours. I learnt a lot in that Fulham cellar in the 1940s. Hopefully I won't forget most of it.

Licentious Rites On Putney Heath

In 1948, I read J. D. Salinger's *Catcher in the Rye* and was completely transfixed by it — a classic novel of teenage angst in America that seemed to strike a chord among so many young people in England at the same time.

Although only thirteen years of age, I found fascinating parallels with my own life in Salinger's brilliant depiction of the prejudices, deep fears and sexual confusion that were all part of the passage from childhood to growing up. The book is full of dark humour and haunting allegories. I was particularly smitten by the hero, Holden Caulfield's description of a "perv", or a sexual deviant as a man who kept a woman's knickers inside his hat.

Inside his hat!

I found this kick-started my imagination into a blaze of fantasy.

After I'd finished *Catcher in the Rye*, I passed it on to Brian Davis who lived in Ringmer Avenue.

He read it and passed it on to Bernard Pendry who in turn gave it to Cynthia, twin sister of Sylvia, who lived a few doors away in Ringmer Avenue.

Apparently Cynthia's mother became suspicious when she found her twelve year-old daughter poring over the by now dog-eared copy of Salinger's book and insisted on reading it first.

I cannot recall Cynthia's mum's reaction, but the book was returned to me a few days later via Bernard and it is probable that Cynthia herself didn't get around to reading it either. It wasn't just American novels that were influencing our young lives in Fulham in the 1940s. Apart from a few bland offerings from J. Arthur Rank or the Ealing Comedy Studios, most movie blockbusters were American. Pop music too was largely transatlantic and it was considered "cool", although that wasn't the word we used, to adopt Americanisms in speech and appearance.

I was inordinately proud of the fact that I could use the word "grand" instead of thousand: it made me seem excruciatingly sophisticated.

Thirteen was also an age of sexual awakening, late by today's standards perhaps, but in 1948 we were not blitzed with sexually provocative images from dawn to dusk in advertisements, hoardings and television. Those early sexual stirrings were accompanied, paradoxically, by a great naivety as we struggled to overcome the mixed feelings of excitement, curiosity and guilt.

One blustery April day, it must have been on a Saturday, six Fulham lads, including myself, boarded a 74 bus and travelled over Putney Bridge and up to the edge of Wimbledon Common, then called Putney Heath. Alighting at the Green Man pub, the end of the route, we trudged for a mile or so across the springy turf, through a stand of silver birches and into a clearing.

I cannot now remember whether the spot was chosen by one of our number or just stumbled into by chance. Our purpose however, was pre-planned. We were all thirteen or fourteen, all six of us, and we had arrived at this quasi-rural idyll for one purpose and one purpose alone. To masturbate as a group. Six lads, all friends, formed a ragged circle facing inwards and with great solemnity, unbuttoned our flies and took out our flaccid penises. It took some time before everybody achieved what passed as an erection, although one boy, a red head with a very white skin, only managed to achieve a half-mast position in spite of the most vigorous efforts of his right hand.

A certain amount of giggling took place and one of the boys passed a copy of *Razzle* around the ranks to stimulate imagination. Most of us found it difficult to hold the magazine steady with our left hand while manipulating our penises with the other.

Two lads refused the offer of *Razzle* preferring to close their eyes and conjure up images of their own invention. It was a curious, extraordinary sight, bizarre even. Six boys, quite unselfconsciously masturbating at varying speeds and differing degrees of intensity.

A couple were languid, performing slow, practised strokes, while others grew frantic, their fists a blur. I think one of the original plans was to see who could "finish" first. To our great surprise, Ginger, he of the horizontal erection, was a clear winner. With a triumphant squeak, he sent an arc of white semen soaring over the grass.

Nobody applauded.

Nobody could.

One by one, we finished. I was a bit slow finding the images of my choosing, they were constantly fading and being replace by a vivid picture of a man's hat stuffed full of women's knickers, which acted as a de-tumescent rather than a stimulant. Damn J. D. Salinger!

When we were at last all done and re-buttoned, there followed an erudite discussion about the degree of pleasure each one of us had experienced ranging from "great" to "smashing". Sid thought his was smashing, Ginger claimed he'd had better at home alone and most of us thought it pretty good, if not exactly "smashing".

There was no hint of sexual interplay between any of the boys that day; nobody touched anybody else: none of us, I venture to recall, displayed any signs of sexual longing for any of the other boys. But I could be wrong. For all I know, that extraordinary display of carnal exhibitionism could well have confirmed an otherwise unformed sexuality into a pattern that became established for life.

What I do remember, was the degree of unselfconscious comradeship we all enjoyed that blustery day. There were no feelings of guilt. Just a quiet satisfaction in discovering that we weren't alone in the world in enjoying the secret pleasures our young bodies could provide.

100

While we waited for the bus to take us back to Fulham, Ginger posed a fascinating question. "Do you think girls do it?" he asked.

We all pondered this deep conundrum solemnly. Finally I offered an answer; bold as brass and based on absolutely zero knowledge of the matter. "Course they do," I said.

"I bet they don't," said Ginger. "I asked my sister about it once. She told Mum I was talking dirty."

"Why don't you ask Helen," said one boy, one of the early finishers. Helen was my current girl friend.

The thought of even raising the subject filled me with a sudden surge of terror. I resolved there and then that I would never ask Helen such a dreadfully intimate and personal question. But, naturally enough, I said, "Yes, I will ask Helen."

"When?" asked Ginger, he of the premature ejaculation.

"When I next see her," was my haughty reply.

Of course I never did. Helen was an exceedingly prim and proper thirteen year old, always neatly dressed with spotless white ankle socks and a perfectly pleated gymslip. Mind you, if I had asked her, how would I have phrased it. In those days we didn't use the word masturbation and if we had, Helen wouldn't have known what it meant.

There was no repeat of the juvenile bacchanalia on Putney Heath, at least as far as I was concerned. It was an event, a "happening" perhaps, another stitch in the great tapestry of adolescence although that in itself sounds gumshrinkingly pretentious.

One thing I can remember about that day, with crystal clear clarity. On a brisk, windy day in April, all little boys who unbutton themselves in the open air are absolutely and completely equal.

Air-Raids

Our flat in Hestercombe Avenue was only a few miles from Battersea Power Station and during the war, according to the *Daily Express*, it was a major target for Hitler's Luftwaffe. By crippling this vital installation, the German High Command believed they could destabilise London's infrastructure and ultimately subjugate the population.

While they never achieved a direct hit on the power station, they came close and a few of their less well-aimed bombs landed in Fulham. The Borough received a fair share of German hits, both high-explosive and incendiary, and many homes were destroyed.

As a nine year old, I found air-raids very exciting indeed. The siren would go off, issuing its mournful warning wail and mother would bundle me and my sister downstairs into the cellar.

Later during the war, we were evacuated to Hall Green in Birmingham, but father stayed in London to perform his police duties. In the early months of the Blitz, however, we all remained at 4 Hestercombe.

If Dad was on night duty when the siren sounded, my mother, sister and I would sit in the cellar with mad Kate and her park keeper husband, Jack. The routine we observed had been fully rehearsed, especially during night raids. Clad in dressing gowns and slippers and clutching blankets, we would descend the wooden steps into the stone-floored cellar where we would sit on cushions on the lower steps. As the cellar was used to store coal, there was always a strong smell of coal dust hanging in the air, and nearly 60 years on, whenever I smell it, I am back on the bottom steps of the Hestercombe cellar eating bread dipped in warm milk and listening to the crump and crack of incendiary bombs dropping, as some did, right in our street just a few doors away.

Mother had bought me a tin helmet in Woolworths for 2/6d and I wore this with the elastic strap firmly under my chin, although I doubt if the thin metal would have been of the slightest protection if the house had collapsed on us during a raid.

Most nights, we could hear the deafening roar of British ack-ack guns in Bishop's Park blazing away at the night sky. Although Dad said they never hit anything; they just made a lot of noise to boost local morale.

Mum never showed that she was nervous, although she must have been, and Mary, my sister, was equally stoic, sitting there in a hair net and eating bars of Cadbury's Dairy Milk chocolate.

Once, when an incendiary landed on the roof of a house opposite, it stuck in a gutter and went off at half-cock like a damp firework. When the "all clear" had sounded, a piercing up-beat note, we all rushed upstairs and went into the street. Flames were shooting from the house opposite and two firemen, already on the scene, had scrambled from their fire engine and were unfurling a long, white hose. People were appearing at all the front doors: women with their hair in curlers, men in pyjamas and working men's boots hastily pulled on and still unlaced, children clutching teddy bears and fluffy rabbits.

Mrs. Humphreys, a formidable battle-axe of a woman who worked in "service" and was married to a dance band drummer called Jack, appeared in a flowing kimono-type gown covered in puce roses and a hair net. She shook a fist at the night sky, her eyes blazing behind the blue-tinted glasses she always wore. "Bastards!" she screamed and we all cheered. "Bastards!" she repeated. Then Jack, her husband, appeared, a small, wiry Liverpudlian who seemed dwarfed by his wife. "Buckingham-bleeding-Palace-sodding-Road!" she suddenly yelled.

"What?" said Jack, pulling his beige cardigan tightly over his orange and white striped pyjamas.

"They aimed at Buckingham-bleeding-Palace-sodding-Road!" screamed "Blue Eyes", as she was fondly known by the neighbours.

"Well," murmured Jack in his Scouser drawl, "They fucking missed, didn't they?"

The fire was quickly doused and the fireman, to great cheers from everybody in the street, leapt aboard their big, shiny, red fire engine and sped off, presumably to some other scene of emergency.

After the all clear, most nights we'd be allowed to stay up and listen to the radio if it wasn't too late.

Sometimes, old Mrs. Gear and her hairdresser husband from next door, would come in and sit in the cellar with us during a raid. Mr. Gear was always fully dressed in street clothes, a suit and polished shoes, whereas old Mrs. Gear, still groggy from a stroke, shuffled in wearing a long, woollen nightie and what appeared to be football socks in Chelsea colours.

During one of the earlier air-raids, when I was about seven, we hadn't got ourselves down into the cellar when the bombs started falling and Dad, who was at home, fearful of a direct hit, crouched over my sleeping form, protecting me with his body in case the roof caved in. But nothing happened. I was not aware of this at the time. Years later, I thanked him and gave him a hug.

On the mornings after an air-raid, we would go into the street and look for shrapnel, jagged bits of metal from the ack-ack guns usually. I collected about six pounds in weight of shrapnel and kept it in cocoa tins in the cellar.

Later on in the war, we had the V1s or doodle-bugs. Now, they were frightening — great ponderous rockets fired from across the Channel that would cut out their motors when they were above their targets. Then followed an eerie silence, a few seconds only, before the screaming sound of descent as they fell, nose first, onto the buildings below. Finally there would be the roar of an explosion and the crash of masonry — ghastly sounds I can still hear today.

We all kept buckets of sand and stirrup-pumps in the hall in case of fire. I thought this was great fun, but I was never allowed to touch the stirrup-pump. I never knew why.

Dad had a gun in his bedroom in case a German parachutist landed in our little garden. Well, it was a pistol actually, a small weapon that had belonged to my grandfather when he was a quartermaster sergeant in India in 1880. It fired small, round balls about the size of a marble. Dad never used it, at least not on any German parachutist. But he did fire it in the garden once. It was deadly accurate up to ten yards. Any distance beyond that and it was likely to miss by a mile.

I've still got it, but it no longer works. The firing mechanism, the pin and the little tray for the gunpowder charge have long since gone.

Some householders in Fulham had shotguns and after an air-raid, when neighbours gathered in little knots in the street, tales would be exchanged about various "sightings" of German soldiers or airmen who had been scampering over the Fulham rooftops yelling "Sieg heil" or, even more improbably, "Die, English svine!"

There is no record of a German landing in Fulham throughout the war and even if one had, I am certain that the local people would have refrained from performing summary executions.

I know what my mother would have done if a Jerry had dropped into our back yard. She would have given him a good smack and then offered him a cup of tea. "He's somebody's son," she would have said, before handing him over to the local ARP warden.

The wardens, with their official armbands and dark blue steel helmets, exuded an air of great importance as they walked the Fulham streets. Many were ex-soldiers who, although too old for military service, were still keen to "do their bit".

One in particular, I remember, was a retired regimental sergeant major who had served in the 1914–18 war. He took his role as warden very seriously indeed: boots polished to a high sheen, white moustache clipped and bristling, he would march along Hestercombe Avenue carrying his walking stick at the trail, like a rifle, and barking out commands in a parade ground voice. "Number seven!" he would bellow, "Put that light out. Don't you know there's a war on?"

After any air-raid, whether by night or day, there would be a surge of community feeling among local residents, a sense that we were "all in this together", a real conviction that as long as we remained united, we would never be beaten. Even as a child, Churchill's wartime speeches broadcast by the BBC made the hairs on the nape of my neck bristle. Whenever the, national anthem was played on the radio at 4 Hestercombe, my mother and father would stand up — a quiet display of patriotism that today would be sneered at as simple-minded and jingoistic.

They were strange days, those 1940s, when the feeling of Britishness and stout defiance were intermingled. They certainly left a mark on me and others of my generation, a mark that many of us are proud to possess even in the first years of this crazy 21st century.

Saturday Night At The Hammersmith Palais

The Hammersmith Palais was a dance hall situated, not surprisingly, just by Hammersmith Broadway. In the late 1940s and early 1950s, Hammersmith was not a salubrious area. Mean streets led off the Broadway past the green towards Shepherd's Bush which was even less salubrious than Hammersmith.

The Palais, however, was a glitter palace ringed with lights that offered working-class boys and girls a whiff of spurious glamour on a Saturday night.

The resident band was led by Ken Mackintosh, a cheery man with a thin black moustache. The early predecessors of modern bouncers hovered at the Palais entrance. They wore Burton's suits with wide lapels and RAF ties. Their shoes were black lace-ups and their trousers hung two inches above the rim of their shoes. They had what my father called military haircuts, short back and sides, so short in fact you could see their scalps showing through the shorn locks.

They presented a vivid contrast to the boys who patronised the Palais on a Saturday night. Most of them wore a uniform that consisted of suits with draped jackets that reached almost to their knees and little string ties nesting against white shirts with long, spear-point collars. Some of them, daringly, had velvet collars which seemed to attract dandruff and cigarette ash. Sometime later, the press dubbed these lads Teddy Boys. They wore their hair slicked back with Brylcreem and swept round behind their heads in ducks-tails.

Inside the Palais, under a revolving glass globe, several hundred young people gathered, mostly separated into groups of males and females, although quite a few came as couples.

The girls favoured very tight "pencil" skirts that covered their knees and the restrictions of the garment made them walk in a curious hobbling shuffle. Shoes were stiletto-heeled and the seamed stockings often sported floral patterns embroidered around the lower calf. Make-up was thick, and many a youthful skin condition was successfully camouflaged by an application of orange-coloured pancake. This cosmetic was dispensed from a small tin kept inside a glitzy handbag and was used to provide running repairs throughout the evening. Hair was rarely worn loose around the shoulders, although fans of Veronica Lake, the American film star, such as myself, preferred the sultry style she had perfected with a curtain of shiny soft hair hanging over half her face. The Palais girls, however, were drawn to the heavily lacquered beehive style where coils of hair were piled into a domed shape and seemed to defy the rule of gravity. I once touched a girl's hair at the Palais, in a sophisticatedly affectionate gesture, and it was like making contact with a coil of damp liquorice.

110

Ken Mackintosh's band were absolutely tremendous. Lots of brass, fruity saxophones and trumpets, jazzy piano and twanging strings. They were the "big band" sound writ large.

The actual dancing that took place was highly ritualised. Unlike today, couples didn't stand two feet apart and gyrate like spastic chimpanzees. They took their partners in a clinch, hip-to-hip and thigh-to-thigh. Even though the dance-fare was composed of the "big 3" — waltz, foxtrot and quickstep — cool youngsters of that era moved at much the same speed for each of these dances in a ponderous movement known as "the creep". The boy would place his left arm around the girl's waist and pull her in close — this ensured snug contact and enabled the boy to press his adolescent erection against her belly with a certain amount of legitimacy. His right hand would hold the girl's left and both would be kept hanging low at their sides. Thus entwined, the dancing would commence. The slow, sensuous shuffle around the polished parquet beneath the shimmering globe was an erotic experience second to none.

The creeping movement was made easier by the boy's mode of footwear, where aficionados of style wore shoes with soles of thick crêpe rubber. It seemed *de rigueur* to sport shoes a size too large so that the general image was of drainpipe-trousered skinny legs feeding into immense, boat-like shoes with a rind of marzipan on the under-sole.

The daring among us could also place his cheek against his partner's pancaked face and chance a crafty ear nibble during the circumnavigation of the sprung dance floor.

Occasionally, the band would play a particularly jazzy number and show-off members of the pack would jive extravagantly, slinging their partners around like sacks of rice or stuffed dolls.

I favoured the creep, especially with pretty girls who let you hold them close and seemed unconcerned with my lack of sartorial elegance. No draped jacket for me, nor alas a pair of suede brothel creepers. Usually it was a Dunn's sports coat and fake cavalry twill pants plus exceedingly naff shoes with Phillips stick-a-soles hiding the holes underneath.

Drinks were almost exclusively non-alcoholic, Coke and Pepsi being the favourite choices. Lads in the building trade, aristocrats of labour, were the ones who treated their girl friends to Pepsi's with an ice cream floating on top. This was excruciatingly sophisticated and the envy of us lads still at school whose finances rarely ran beyond a lemonade.

Nobody arrived by car. Trolley buses would decant would-be revellers from as far afield as Battersea or even rural Putney, although the Putney crowd had the opportunity of patronising the equally glitzy Wimbledon Palais where smart opinion had it that the girls were more likely to permit liberties after the dance than their London counterparts. Big Georgie Hughes, the bodybuilding colossus whose mum owned a second-hand furniture shop in Fulham, was of the considered opinion that Wimbledon girls were sex-crazed because of the bracing Surrey air whereas in smoky

Hammersmith, factory fumes and motor bike exhausts diluted the female libido something chronic. Georgie Hughes knew a thing or two about life, of that there was no doubt.

There was rarely any serious trouble at the Hammersmith Palais, apart from the occasional scuffle between two brothel — kreepered lads over the affections of a girl. Assignations would often be made at the bus station after the dance and many a youthful romance was ignited while waiting for a 30 bus bound for Hackney Wick.

I smoked my first full cigarette at Hammersmith Palais at the age of fifteen and, contrary to popular myth, I didn't turn green or throw up, but found the experience mildly enjoyable.

It was a Capstan Full Strength, untipped, a brand that, if it existed today and were being smoked by a minor, would cause eruptions of disgust and horror by social workers, *Guardian* readers and other balls-aching do-gooders. In 1950, a Capstan Full Strength was as potent a passport to manhood as full intercourse without your socks on with an older woman who wore suspenders.

The Palais was where young boys, scarcely out of short trousers, realised that girls were not only different, but from another planet. It was at the Palais that I first clapped eyes on an early love of my life a petite blonde with eyes of cornflower blue and tiny, exquisite ears and a waist you could span with both hands. She bounced as she walked and to dance with her was a visit to Shangri-La.

Unfortunately, she was in such demand that I was obliged to admire her from afar for three whole Saturdays before I got to dance with her myself. Then the illusion was shattered when she spoke her first words to me. What she actually said I cannot recall, but it was something trivial. What delivered the hammer blow was the voice. How best to describe it? A chalk being drawn across slate perhaps. Or Alf Garnett before he had elocution lessons. Ripe is the word. Ripe. She was lovely, but the voice was too much, even for a boy as desperate as I was for fun and romance.

I shall treasure my memories of the Hammersmith Palais. It was part of my rite of passage to the brave new world of the 1950s.

Bathtime, Books and Stories

Between 1945 and 1953, when I joined the army to do my stint of National Service, we had no television set at Hestercombe Avenue nor, as far as I can recall, did any of our neighbours, not even the patrician Mr. Gear, hairdresser to Whites Club, up West.

Radio was our main source of entertainment, although we called it the wireless in those days.

Unlike today, with the proliferation of portables, we had just one set, a huge brown juggernaut with wire mesh covering the dials and round knobs for controlling the volume and the wavelength. It sat on a stout table in our back room and it was here, in dressing gown and slippers, clutching a glass of Horlicks, that I consumed many hours of old BBC dramas.

H. G. Wells' *War of the Worlds* adapted for radio, the spine-chilling *Appointment with Fear*, the daily fix of *Dick Barton Special Agent* a fifteen-minute burst of frenzied derring-do where public school educated Dick vanquished countless villains, mostly foreign, often from fly-blown Levantine corners of the earth, assisted by proletarian chums Jock, Scot and Snowy, a lovable Cockney.

There was, of course, *Paul Temple*, a more cerebral crime fighter, and this series had a particularly memorable theme tune, "Coronation Scot".

115

However, casting aside any nostalgic pretensions, it is fair to say that much radio fare on offer in the 1940s was unspeakably dire.

My parents loved Tommy Handley in his famous show *ITMA*, but I found it buttock-clenchingly unfunny.

Sunday lunchtimes were usually accompanied by a record request programme, *Two-Way Family Favourites*, on which dedications were read out from families to their sons serving in the army overseas, and vice-versa. This was followed by a feast of down-market, but harmless, banality and music that was the aural equivalent of a cheeky seaside postcard. It was called, *The Billy Cotton Bandshow*, and it was a hugely popular programme.

On the occasion of a major international boxing tournament, my father and I would crouch around the wireless set and listen to the famous Raymond Glendenning giving a blow-by-blow account of the bout. Glendenning, a magnificently moustached, gung-ho sort of man, was a superb commentator. He could paint vivid word pictures that made you feel you were ringside beside him, seeing the sweat fly and feeling the thwack of leather on human flesh.

Inter-round commentaries were provided by a man called W. Barrington Dalby, another well-spoken toff who, I seem to recall, invariably got it all wrong. "I think the coloured boy's got him worried," he would confidently announce between rounds four and five. "It's all over now for the Belgian [his opponent] bar the shouting."

Round five of course would see the "coloured boy" knocked unconscious with a hammer blow and the Belgian's hand raised in victory.

When I went to see my first boxing match, live at the Walham Green Baths some years later, it wasn't half as enjoyable as hearing it on the wireless. Even though I earned my living in the television industry for 30 years, I still think radio is my preferred medium as a consumer. As my father once said, it's "mind food" and I think that's a pretty good description.

I also haunted the Fulham Library, a dull, silent place where to speak above a whisper was a hanging offence, but let loose among those shelves, riffling through those delicious volumes, touching the leather-bound spines of some of the more esoteric works, opening pages, devouring paragraphs or whole chapters at random, I was in my element.

At home, of course, there were Father's bedtime stories, products of his remarkably fertile imagination. Father's tales were almost exclusively of the "heroic deeds of Empire" variety and the fiction was supplemented by true stories about his father, my grandfather, who served in the late 19th century in the King's Royal Rifle Corps.

Grandfather, a colour-sergeant of dashing appearance with a magnificent handlebar moustache, won campaign medals in India, Burma and South Africa. He was born in 1852, the same year that the Duke of Wellington died. Grandad died when I was six months old, so I never met him. Occasionally, after a particularly riveting tale of Grandad's adventures

117

among the heathens, my father would go down to the cellar and bring up the "black box".

This was a carefully observed family ritual because inside the black box were souvenirs and artefacts gathered by my grandfather during his 22 years in the service of the British Empire: Gurkha knives, curved and gleaming, which I was only allowed to handle in the presence of an adult, old snuff boxes with regimental crests embossed on the lid, beaded Zulu headbands, an old army pistol, several pieces of carved ivory from Indian temples, exquisitely detailed; tiny wagons being pulled by oxen, all carved by hand.

One item, too large to be kept in the box, was a carved wooden figure of Buddha, sitting cross-legged with an expression of benign solemnity. We christened her "Lizzie" although she's clearly a male, and today she sits in my hall in Surrey, a silent guardian of ancient secrets, a mute link between today and the lost world of empire and the 19th century. Also hanging in my hall today is Grandfather's magnificent dress sword in its leather scabbard with brass casing. I regard this as something of an icon to be passed from father to son, from generation to generation. Both my son, Gregory, and my grandson, Daniel, will own it eventually.

Storytelling was an art my father perfected and it didn't really matter that he often edited or even re-wrote some of the classics when telling them to us in abbreviated form.

The best night for stories was Friday, if Dad wasn't on night duty, because Friday was bath night at Hestercombe Avenue. The only bathroom in the whole house was on the landing of the first floor and we shared it with Mr. and Mrs. Bailey — "mad Kate" and her dour park-keeper husband, Jack Bailey, a taciturn Geordie who tolerated her eccentric outbursts with saintly rectitude.

A ritual was closely observed on bath nights. A galvanised tin bath about the size of a child's cot would be filled with water and placed on top of the gas stove in Mother's tiny scullery — no way could it have been described as a kitchen. It had a stone floor, a sink, a wooden draining board, the gas oven and a mangle. That was it. Today, the owners of Hestercombe Avenue probably treat it as a little corridor leading to the yard outside.

After the tin bath had sat on the gas jets for about ten minutes, steam and bubbles would appear. Father would shake in a generous portion of soda crystals "to soften the water" and then test the temperature by putting in his hand up to the elbow. Then the tin bath would be carried upstairs by either my mother and father or, when I was eleven, me and my father, and the whole steaming, soda-saturated load would be poured in a great swoosh into the bath proper. This was a deep iron receptacle with claw feet at each corner. We bathed in strict reverse order of seniority, youngest first, oldest last.

I would plunge into the grey water, which because of the added soda, had the appearance of a stagnant pool. My bath took less than five minutes. Speed was of the essence as the water tended to lose its embracing warmth in a house without central heating. My sister would follow, then mother and finally, into that glistening effluvia, my father.

The only lavatory available to our family and the Baileys was in that bathroom and I have always believed that the speed at which our family bathed in those days was prompted by the double pressures of the water's losing its temperature and an unspoken fear that Mrs. Bailey might at any moment burst in and tear down her voluminous bloomers and squat on the loo.

We, on the other hand, had our own exclusive loo outside the house in the yard. It could easily have doubled as a cold store, even in summer. My father once painted the wooden seat with a kind of early creosote which took ages to dry. I displayed the tell-tale signs of creosote rings on my shirt tails for months. Only after half a dozen or more emersions in Mum's sink full of suds did the stains vanish.

My father had joined a book club and each month a new hardback would arrive by post which, after my father had read it, was passed to me. Most of the volumes were thrillers, John Cheyney, Agatha Christie, Warwick Deeping, but I devoured them all, reading them in conjunction with my childish fare of Enid Blyton and Arthur Ransome.

At the Fulham Library, I borrowed American novelists: Steinbeck, Hemingway, O'Hara, Irwin Shaw. O'Henry and Edgar Allan Poe came later. Racier fare with heavy sexual overtones by writers such as Hank Jansen, I had to borrow from my friend Sid who was a devotee.

The Fulham Library didn't acknowledge that Hank Jansen even existed. When I once asked for a Jansen title at the library, the librarian, a caricature of all fictional librarians ever invented, a lady with a faint grey moustache, brown, uneven teeth and a mauve pullover, sniffed dismissively. I think she knew in her heart of hearts that Hank Jansen, if he were in fact really a living person, would inevitably have been a purveyor of smutty literature. One of my favourite books was called *Limehouse Nights*, a tale of gaslit London where secret gangs of Chinese opium smokers constantly evaded arrest. I think it was the imagery of Victorian London, the mean streets of Jack the Ripper, that so fascinated me.

When I joined the Shakespeare Society at my grammar school, it was my headmaster, Guy Boas, who introduced me to Dickens, Thackeray and of course the bard himself.

My proudest moment was playing Salanio in *The Merchant of Venice*. W. Darlington, the old *Daily Telegraph* theatre critic, thought our school production, directed by Guy Boas, was "dangerously professional".

How nostalgic it is to recall those days and remind ourselves that now we all have a great future behind us.

Hair

Jack Risk, the barber, had a salon in the Munster Road. He was also a neighbour of ours in Hestercombe Avenue where he lived with his wife Gladys and five daughters.

Jack Risk was a short-back-and-sides merchant by instinct and was thus approved of by my father who believed devoutly that a "military haircut" was next to godliness.

However, in the late 1940s, a trend had drifted over to England from the United States. It was wholly reprehensible of course, like most things from that part of the world. It was called *style*. Particularly when applied to the way in which young men had their hair cut.

Photographs began to appear in the window of Jack Risk's salon. Dangerously subversive pictures they were too. They depicted various American film stars showing off their very personal hair styles. There was the Tony Curtis — a firm favourite: sleek at the sides and gleaming with hair oil and with a small knot of curls in the front that stood like a bunch of grapes on the forehead. Then there was the Alan Ladd: a soft curtain of hair hanging limply over one eyebrow. The Cornel Wilde: a riot of curls that ended with a bunch of the stuff hanging over the collar at the back. The Bela Lugosi — not a great favourite, but daring and different: hair plastered to the scalp and parted in the middle as if a tomahawk had been deftly applied to Mr. Lugosi's cranium.

I particularly lusted after the Tony Curtis and one day, clutching my shilling, I asked Jack Risk to give me a Tony Curtis.

He smiled his toothy smile and pulled his scissors from the top pocket of his off-white smock. "Your Dad says short back and sides, son. Sorry that's it."

There was no point in remonstrating with Jack Risk even though I offered an extra sixpence. "Look," said Jack kindly, "you need to grow you hair first. I couldn't give you a Tony Curtis even if I wanted to. Know what I mean?" I said, "I'll grow it."

"Better ask your dad first," said Jack and proceeded to snip at my scalp with his fingers moving in a blur.

In five minutes, I climbed from the chair having had my head squirted with a setting lotion that solidified like industrial lacquer. My haircut was very short. Lots of white scalp showing through what was left of my auburn locks.

On the way out of Jack's salon, I eyed the picture of Tony Curtis with anguished longing.

Some of the older boys in Fulham, that is to say boys of fifteen or sixteen, had already anticipated the American trend and sported the infamous D/A haircut. At the merest suggestion that I should let my hair grow in order to try out one of the new styles, my father came over all militant and disapproving. "You let your hair grow too long and you weaken it," was his famous statement. "And all that oil," he would add, shuddering, "Fleas love it."

It occurred to me that I might point out that a blob of Brylcreem was more likely to drown a flea or suffocate it than provide it with nourishment, but I thought better of it.

"And furthermore," Dad would sometimes add in a tone of moral finality, "I don't trust men who ponce themselves up like tarts."

So that was it. No prospect of a Tony Curtis or a D/A or even a Bela Lugosi at fourteen years of age.

My friend, Sid, who had an even spottier forehead than I was allowed by his parents to have a fringe. This limp curtain of black hair was there to hide some of his more volcanic blemishes, but somehow it didn't make him look remotely like Alan Ladd.

Big Georgie Hughes, the bodybuilder from Walham Green whose Mum had a second-hand furniture shop, had naturally curly, blonde hair which he wore quite long. His style was almost a perfect replica of the classic Tony Curtis except Curtis was dark haired.

Doug Wilson, my friend, a later training partner at St. George's weightlifting club, had shiny black hair, — very glossy and well groomed. He knew of a shop in Hammersmith where you could buy false sideburns for eleven pence. They always found a pair, apparently, that matched your own hair colour exactly. All very well, but *eleven pence*! Completely out of order as far as I was concerned.

124

A boy called Wheeler who lived in Ringmer Avenue, next to our street, started going bald at the age of fifteen — alopecia or something similar, my mother said. It did clear up in the end, but not before whispers had circulated among his friends that his hair loss was due to excessive wanking.

Masturbation was very popular among lads in Fulham. We showed contempt for the warnings that it might impair your eyesight or grow fur on the palms of our hands. We called it "tossing-off". Older boys with a *soupçon* of sophistication called it, "the five fingered widow".

Unscheduled erections could also pose a problem for young boys still in short trousers. Sitting on the top of a bus was particularly tricky. The bouncing motion always set you off. Nothing you could do would stop that flow of blood to the loins. Many a time, I had to cover my embarrassment with my school cap when alighting from a number 14 bus.

If I'd been allowed to have a Tony Curtis haircut, things would have been different. People would have been too busy admiring my coiffure to notice any priapic protuberance.

After-The-War-Cake And Other Delights

Rabbit was a regular staple of our diet at Hestercombe Avenue. Mother used to cook it in a large saucepan and serve it in big slices with potatoes and cabbage. I remember the rabbit bones were small and brittle and you could break them easily between your front teeth.

My sister liked rabbits, so did I, but we regarded them as pets, little fluffy things you could cuddle and play with. So initially, while we were very young, mother used to serve rabbit stew and say, "It's just meat. Like chicken."

For some years, we believed her. We ate rabbit because we thought it was chicken meat, or some sort of unnamed poultry. By the time we knew it was rabbit, we didn't care. I discovered it by chance one day when I had been sent to the butcher's to buy some sliced bacon. I saw them hanging up in the shop on metal hooks, skinned. They looked like cats, so I asked, "Are those things cats?"

The butcher, who had huge red hands with fingers the size of his pork sausages and a nose cratered with open pores and threaded with blue veins, laughed morosely. "Cats! No boy, they's rabbit. From

126

Berkshire." Why he had to tell me their place of origin escapes me, but the awful truth was out. We'd been eating rabbit for years. I rushed home and blurted out the facts to my mother and sister.

Mother deployed all of her Wiltshire cunning when confronted with this dramatic dénouement. "I never said they were chickens," she said, "and I never said they weren't rabbits. I said they were *like* chicken meat." Fleshy white strips of meat nestling in pale gravy, they certainly didn't look like rabbits: no fluffy tails, no long floppy ears. They were indeed just like "chicken meat".

Now, today, they are back in fashion. What goes around comes around.

The food we ate in 1948 and through the very early 1950s would today be condemned as grossly incorrect. Dietitians of the 1990s would swoon in horror at our domestic bill of fare: butter, eggs, milk, fatty meat, suet puddings, lashings of white sugar; salad, almost never. And the word cholesterol had yet to be invented. Mother's speciality was suet pudding cooked in a cloth which was tied at both ends before it was shoved into the pot. It would emerge, steaming, an hour later and the string holding the ends would be snipped and the pudding released from its restraining cloth. There it would sit, a great white, glutinous dollop, all slimy on the outside and light and fluffy on the inside. Over this smoking lump of suet, golden syrup would be drizzled or, if none were available, white sugar by the heaped spoonful.

For tea on Saturdays, my sister and I would feast on white bread and dripping. Now, beef dripping is simply liquid fat that slowly oozes from a hunk of meat and drips into a bowl, often through a muslin cloth. When it sets, it looks like frozen candle wax, but softer. Spread generously on doorstep-sized hunks of bread and liberally salted, it is absolute bliss. To consume dripping today would be considered an act of suicide.

My all time favourite, however, was Mum's rice pudding. This was made in a large dish with blue edging and, before it was placed in the oven, nutmeg would be grated over its surface. The pudding itself was loaded with cream and huge lumps of butter before it was cooked.

When it emerged with its brown skin steaming, we would spoon generous helpings on our plates and then plop great blobs of jam or marmalade on it and presto, the ultimate Babylonian feast!

As a snack, I favoured condensed milk sandwiches sprinkled with brown sugar or, when they were available after the war, bananas and chocolate spread. The phrase, "after the war" has great resonance with me as during that great conflict, many foodstuffs simply didn't appear in the shops.

There was food rationing, and when we asked our mother for cake with fruit and currants instead of the plain stuff we had in 1946 — cakes we'd seen in photographs in American magazines — she would say, "that's after-the-war-cake". And true to her word, when rationing finished, she made fruit cakes of Olympic proportions.

To this day, I still refer to rich fruit cake as "after-the-war-cake". Old habits die hard.

During the early 1940s, there was an egg shortage, or at least we assumed there was. Instead of the real thing, Mum used to buy dried eggs. They came in waxed cartons from America and they were a special treat. Inside, was a yellow powder which, when added to water, would cook up splendidly into a kind of rubbery omelette.

I must now confess, in my middle 1960s, that I think dried egg tasted a hell of a lot better than the battery-produced jobs we consume today. As somebody once said, "You can take the lad out of Fulham, but you sure as hell can't take Fulham out of the lad!"

Hooray For Dr. Edith

In 1949, the Labour Party's local office was in Harold Laski House at the junction of the Munster and Fulham roads.

Just along from Harold Laski House were the sprawling premises of Claude Rye, the motor cycle retailer and bold exponent of capitalist free enterprise.

Laski House was a bleak, pinched-looking, modern building with morally uplifting posters in the window, some of which were of Clem Atlee, the Prime Minister, a weedy, bald-headed man with the demeanour of a provincial bank clerk.

Claude Rye, in stark contrast, had huge posters of exotic motor bikes in the window, great gleaming silver and black machines with girls in billowing skirts leaning against them, showing their stocking tops.

Directly opposite Claude Rye's Motor Bike Emporium, which covered a complete block, were the premises of the local dentist, a Mr. Painter whose very appearance on the streets struck terror into the hearts of the chocoholics and boiled sweet aficionados who lay thick on the ground in post-war Fulham.

My father, a policeman stationed at Rochester Row in Central London, was, and always had been, a

130

committed, even fanatical, Conservative. Socialism, he maintained, was an aberration, almost an affliction.

One day after school, I saw him sitting at the dining table in our small flat reading the *Fulham Chronicle*, the local paper. He was still half in uniform, serge trousers and big policeman's boots; his helmet was hanging up in the hall. He folded the paper carefully and put it on the table next to the plate of mashed potato and eggs my mother had prepared for him. Then he looked at me with his soft, grey, kind eyes and said, "Do you know who they've got as their member of parliament?" "They", of course, were the local Labour Party.

As a fourteen year old, my knowledge of politics could have been stored in a thimble with room to spare. "No," I said. Not an unreasonable answer under the circumstances.

"Edith Summerskill."

This information left me absolutely cold. He might just as well have told me that it was Tarzan of the Apes or one of the Three Horsemen of the Apocalypse.

My father turned back to his plate of mashed potato and took a steaming forkful. "She wants to ban boxing," he said.

My mother, at that moment, came into the room from the scullery and put a bottle of O.K. sauce in front of my father. He unscrewed the top and held the neck over his mashed potato, then he smacked the base of the bottle with the palm of his other hand. A glob of brown sauce shot out and splashed over the potato.

"No need to do that," said my mother. "I've already shaken it."

"Yes," said my father, ignoring Mother's admonition over the treatment of the sauce bottle, "Yes. She wants to ban boxing. Wrote a book called *The Ignoble Art*. Wants it banned."

"I agree with her," Mother said and wiped her hands on her pinny. She did this even when they were clean. It was an unconscious gesture of emphasis she made when stating an unpopular opinion.

"Well I don't," said my father and swallowed an enormous mouthful of potato. Being mashed, he didn't chew it, but simply gulped it down. "But I admire her."

This remark came as a surprise, even a revelation, as usually when my father spoke of Labour politicians, he spoke of them as if they were the spawn of the devil. "She may be Labour," he said, by way of explanation, "but she's got guts. Standing for Parliament here in Fulham. A woman. If it weren't for the fact that I want Winston Churchill back as prime minister, I'd vote for her."

My mother smiled. I was baffled. Unable to follow the drift of my father's argument, I closed my ears and pretended to listen until my father finished his little speech and went back to his mashed potato and egg.

About a month later, I saw Dr. Edith Summerskill on a street corner near my old primary school, Sherbrooke Road. She was standing on a wooden platform talking to a small crowd of about twenty people, mostly men in cloth caps the majority of whom were smoking. She was a severe-looking woman in a fawn overcoat and a hat with a high brim. She wore a rosette on the lapel of her coat and leather gloves. Her voice was beautifully modulated and, I concluded, extremely posh. This then was the woman my father would have voted for it he hadn't wanted Winston Churchill to be prime minister again.

And she wanted to ban boxing.

It's extraordinary, but when I think of Dr. Edith Summerskill standing on that wooden platform in Fulham wearing the funny hat with the high brim and the fawn overcoat and the leather gloves, even though it was well over 50 years ago, I don't actually see her face or hear her voice in my recalled images, but those of Mrs. Margaret Thatcher. Now there's a strange thing.

Smoke

At the Sloane Grammar School where, in the hyperbolic description by my father, both the sons of dukes and sons of dustmen were educated side-by-side, there were certain divisions. These were not based on class, although we were a little apprehensive about middle-class pupils from Kensington who wore wristwatches and always had clean socks.

The real divisions were based on territorial origins. Fulham lads tended to stick together, while those from Chelsea and Pimlico rubbed shoulders with natives of the same district. Thus in my fourth year, in class 4B, a cluster of Fulham boys would contrive to sit close together like a juvenile mafia. What we had in common, apart from a SW6 address, was a mindlessly fanatical loyalty to Fulham Football Club and a clandestine lust for Capstan Full Strength Untipped cigarettes. Smoking, behind, or even in front of, the legendary bike shed, was one of the rituals of the Fulham tribe.

Although I puffed along with the best of them, I seldom consumed more than two or three fags a day. If that.

The champion, the undisputed smoker in our midst, was a splendid fellow called Gony — not his real name of course. He was a tall, blonde boy who cycled to school, as most of us did, on a red racing bike, a Norman Invader. And he lived in Hammersmith! How come he was part of the Fulham group then?

Well, the block of flats where he lived with his widowed mother, who incidentally was of upper-middle-class stock and spoke like a duchess, was on the very border twixt Fulham and Hammersmith.

When deciding whether Gony should be part of the *Cosa Nostra*, we were ultimately swayed by his extremely close proximity to Fulham and, it has to be said, his generous distribution of cigarettes during break period. Not just Capstan Full Strength either. I was personally the recipient of Craven "A" ("For your throat's sake"), Player's Navy Cut, Piccadilly, Woodbines (a special favourite) and, on very important occasions, even a Cocktail Sobranie, a black fag with a gold band round the tip. I learnt later that there weren't just black cigarettes in the Sobranie stable, but each pack contained a variety of colours! Red, green, blue, etc. What sophistication! What *élan*!

Gony was a most valuable and trusted member of the Fulham gang.

It is perhaps not entirely coincidental that half a century on, Fulham and Hammersmith are now joined together under a single local authority, the Borough of Fulham and Hammersmith. I wonder how many multi-coloured Cocktail Sobranies Gony had to slip to the London borough planners to obtain that magnificent result.

Heroes Of The Young

In the 1940s, the heroes of the young were nothing like the heroes doted on by the youth of today. Take footballers for instance. Today, the star players are just that: stars. They earn prodigious salaries, drive immense automobiles, marry pouting models with golden thighs and breasts that defy gravity, and reside in opulent mansions complete with razored lawns, swimming pools and saunas.

In the 1940s, the football stars were paid working-class wages (salaries were for the middle class), and lived lives of humdrum normality.

I once saw my hero, Ronnie Rooke, Fulham FC's centre forward and prolific goal scorer, queuing outside a fish and chip shop wearing a cloth cap. Can you imagine one of today's stars doing that? Their careers were short, and only a few, like the great Stanley Matthews, had an alternative occupation. In his case, a small hotel in the north of England. If Matthews had reached his prime today, he'd be a multi-millionaire celebrity.

In the 1940s, popular music was mostly American. The British domination of the industry was still a decade and a half away. We liked Frankie Laine, an American with a belter of a voice who sang "Jezebel" as if his life depended on it, and Johnny Ray, another American, a strange fellow with a hearing aid who had a monster hit with a mournful ballad called, "Cry".

The "big band sound" did have a few British musicians making a contribution, like Ted Heath, but our favourites were mostly Yanks like the incredible Stan Kenton and his trumpet who could hit high notes only audible to a dog.

British singers were, on the whole, quite awful; Donald Peers, for example whose signature tune was the grisly song "By a Babbling Brook".

Film star heroes were also American: Alan Ladd, Tony Curtis, Errol Flynn. But they dressed and looked like stars. Not for them the unshaven chin or torn denim of the current crop of overpaid hooligans. Publicity photographs of the Hollywood stars were very stylish, often by Karsh of Ottawa. Hair was immaculate, skin unblemished, suits immaculately cut. These were icons you could look up to.

And they weren't a bit like you. Today, the heroes of the young have a look as dishevelled and gormless as their fans.

We didn't have *Playboy* or *Mayfair* or any of the other skin magazines in the 1940s. Pin-up photographs of glamour girls were quite respectable, the most famous being Betty Grable, posing with her back to you in a bathing suit that came halfway down her thighs. No thong for Betty Grable, no pouting buttock cheeks to inflame the libido of your pre-teen Fulham lads.

If you wanted really sexy pictures, you bought *Razzle*, mild by today's standards, or *Health & Efficiency*, a naturist magazine with curiously un-erotic pictures of young women with permed hair playing beach ball naked, but with their pubic hair blotted out.

There was, of course, *Lilliput* magazine, a splendid journal with erudite articles on a variety of subjects and just one black and white photograph of a nude lady. She was often a lady called Pamela Green, whose bearded husband, Harrison Marks, was the actual photographer. How we envied him. Pamela looked ravishing. He was, well, a man with a beard! There was clearly no justice in the world.

For my part, I had four favourite heroes, two male and two female. The men I looked up to were Errol Flynn (the main reason I grew a moustache at seventeen), and bow-legged Ronnie Rooke, the Fulham centre forward. Mind you, when he left to join Arsenal, I crossed him off my list.

My female icons over whom I lusted hopelessly were Veronica Lake, the blonde American star who peeped from behind a curtain of shiny hair, and the indescribably sexy Barbara Stanwyk. Ye Gods, she wore a tiny gold chain around her ankle in the movie *Double Indemnity* and it drove me mad!!

I watched the video of *Double Indemnity* again recently. Dear old Barbara still has pulling power in spite of the angora sweater and the curious choice of frocks. I would have placed Pamela Green on my list of all time greats, but come on, she was married to a photographer with a beard. This just wasn't cricket, a game, incidentally, which I found incomprehensible and boring even when my girl friend Helen said she was in love with Len Hutton, whoever he was.

First Glimpse Of The Sea

I was eleven years old when I first saw the sea. My primary school, Sherbrooke Road in Fulham, had organised a rare visit by bus to Brighton and although technically I was no longer a pupil there, having just passed my eleven-plus and been admitted to Sloane Grammar School in Chelsea, I persuaded Mum to fork out the half-crown, I think it was, to pay for the trip.

I was familiar with the countryside, having been briefly evacuated to Birmingham during the war, but the English coastline had remained, until now, as remote as Outer Mongolia.

We read comics in the bus on the journey through London and the Sussex countryside: *Beano, Dandy* and some of the more literate among us the *Wizard* and the *Champions*.

As the bus, a requisitioned London Red, approached Brighton sea front, we laid aside our reading material and took notice. The ocean lay stretched out before us, huge and disappointingly grey. All the pictures I had seen of it previously showed it as a mirror-smooth deep blue.

Low clouds, also grey, scudded swiftly across the skyline and a fierce wind had whipped the edges of the

140

sea, where it broke on the pebbled beach into a collar of murky foam. It was a typical July day.

We decanted from the bus, two dozen or so London children, in shorts and woollen jumpers, and were herded into a line.

My first vivid recollection, apart from the greyness of the sea, was the smell. Ozone, salt, wind, a hint of vinegar and an overarching stench of rancid cooking fat. This, I later observed, was merely because we had parked the bus next to a particularly villainous-looking fish and chip shop.

Brighton front in 1946 had the appearance of a city under siege. Many of the shops were boarded up and various bits and pieces of rusting metal still sat on the beach, remnants of invasion obstacles or items of discarded military equipment, so our master, Mr. Downey, told us.

We filed across the main road which separated the great hotels from the beach and promenade and were allowed to look at, but not walk into, the Great Pier — I was impressed with the rusting Victorian latticework which supported the mighty edifice that to an eleven year old's eye seemed to stretch for miles out to sea.

We crunched over the shiny wet pebbles on the beach right down to the water's edge. I dipped a finger into the bubbling spume and licked it. Very salty. Two colleagues followed suit and more would have done so had not Mr. Downey issued a stern rebuke. Various bits of flotsam bobbed in the shallow water. Rotting splinters of wood, cardboard containers, tiny dead fish, swollen cigarette butts. One boy located a used condom, neatly knotted at the top and this caused several seconds of guilty laughter, even from those who hadn't the faintest idea what it was. Mr. Downey hooked up the disgusting object with his walking stick and carried it some yards up the beach to a rusty waste bin into which, with ill-concealed distaste, he deposited it.

A brace of seagulls swooped out of nowhere and raced past us on extended wings, their necks stretched and their tiny feet sticking out at the rear.

We continued along the beach, past upturned rowing boats with peeling paint, until we came to a section separated from the rest by a wooden groyne. This wooden barrier had accumulated strands of slimy green vegetation and to its sides, countless tiny limpets had attached themselves.

Just beyond the groyne, huddled low out of the knife like wind, two young people were eating sandwiches and pouring tea from a thermos flask. The man was wearing a Fairisle sweater of elaborate design, the sort of garment maiden aunts knitted for infrequently seen nephews. The girl was smoking a cigarette at the same time as she chewed on her egg sandwich. It was a feat of dexterity known only to the working class of the immediate post-war era.

We moved on; my legs in the grey shorts now displayed signs of goose-bumps and my nose was running — clear — harbingers of an approaching cold.

After half a mile or so of crunching over the pebbles, Mr. Downey halted us with a wave of his walking stick and pointed out, with what I thought was unnecessary dramatic intonation, the Grand Hotel. It was a very big building with lots of windows.

Mr. Downey waited for the gasps of appreciation that he felt must surely follow his announcements. Harry Collier, a skinny boy who had suffered from rickets, and still had one bony leg in irons, sniffed derisively. It may have been a grand hotel to most people, but to Harry Collier and the rest of us, it looked like the usual forbidden pile we saw in London, and one that the likes of us were not encouraged to enter. I thought it looked like a hospital and I didn't like the way they smelled.

Mr. Downey gave a cluck of disappointment and we moved on in single file. He led us up the beach and onto the promenade. Here a few people sauntered past, one man, very fat and old, was wearing a coat with a large fur collar and was accompanied by a much younger girl in high heeled shoes and stockings with a seam down the back. As they passed, Mr. Downey gave the other teacher, Mr. Lane, a knowing look. More of a leer actually, as I recall. The look spoke, as indeed it was intended to, volumes. However, even at eleven, I had a faint grasp of such subtle nuances of human nature. Later I whispered into the bemused Harry Collier's ear the forbidden word "shagging". I don't think the poor wretch understood me at all, but I felt excruciatingly sophisticated.

We followed Mr. Downey up into the town past shops and little cafes, most of which were closed, and then down again to the beach. It had started raining and the glowering clouds now touched the horizon.

We had been in Brighton just over and hour and Mr Downey consulted his watch. 12.30. Lunch. We filed back to the bus where we had all left our paper bags full of sandwiches, and then we sat in the bus as the rain streamed down the windows, and ate our lunches.

I had cheese and marmite sandwiches and a sponge cake. Harry Collier had two slices of bread and dripping pressed together, of which he only ate half. I gave him a bite of my sponge cake, but he didn't seem to enjoy it.

The rain grew in intensity, pounding on the roof of the bus like machine gun fire and, after a whispered consultation with the driver, Mr. Downey announced that we were heading back to London.

My cold came out with a vengeance later that day and as I sat miserably in front of the radio listening to *Just William* at our flat in Hestercombe Avenue, Mum gave me a cup of tea laced with Famel syrup. "How was Brighton?" she asked.

My reply was considered and uttered with absolute clarity. "I hated it. I never want to go to the seaside again." But of course, I did.

Whatever Happened To Bunny?

Although Fulham in the 1940s was largely a working-class enclave, with most people renting their homes rather than buying them, there existed a few pockets of relative affluence like Hurlingham, where the decidedly up-market Hurlingham Club was located. This was foreign territory to most of us, an almost mythical never-never land which was never visited by scruffs from our end of the borough.

Polo was played at the Hurlingham Club and on Saturdays, shiny black Humber Super-Snipes and SS Jaguars would roll up and glide through the gated entrance into the green acres of the polo grounds. I once saw a horse-box arrive and heard the animal neighing as it was driven into the club.

Another area of middle-class pretension was close to Bishop's Park. This was where the sprawling Key Mansion Flats were situated. Men who lived here wore suits, not overalls or uniforms; shoes, not boots; bowler hats, not cloth caps or Trilbys.

My father was sometimes scathing about the residents of the Key Flats. "Bloody hairdressers mostly," he would say, "made their money flattering silly women and untaxed tips."

Parallel to the road in which the Key Flats had been built, was Harbord Street, a terrace of pretty, but modest houses, smaller then Hestercombe Avenue. One of my closest friends lived in a tiny flat in Harbord Street with his mother and sister. He was called Bunny and his sister was called Bunty. Their surname was Siggers, but we never knew whether their father was dead or just "gone away".

Bunny wore suede shoes and a blazer and played the piano. In their tiny flat, it took up almost all of the "parlour" or back room which served as the main living quarters for the family. Bunny was a tall, skinny boy with hair that was elaborately waved like a 1920s band leader. He spoke in a lazy drawl which was an approximation of what he believed was an upper-class accent. His sister Bunty spoke very nicely too, but at the speed of a machine gun.

They were both destined for better things. Except that twenty years later, I learnt that Bunny had become a prominent member of the local Communist Party and worked energetically for the overthrow of the capitalist system and its replacement by a proletarian dictatorship. The suede shoes and blazer had been consigned to the dustbin of history and Bunny could be spotted on soap boxes the North End Road in a Lenin-type cap, exhorting the local populace to rise up against their oppressors.

I found it hard to reconcile the young swell at the piano, playing elegant tunes by Noel Coward, with the lefty of later years. But then life is always full of surprises. I often wondered what eventually became of him — a charming, witty, handsome boy who could, in my opinion, have reached the top as a night-club pianist or public relations guru.

Then, 50 years on, due to the miracle of the internet and a site called "Friends Reunited", I was able to meet Bunny again. He had worked as a human resources executive, or as I prefer to call it, a personnel executive, for a major pharmaceutical company. At 67 he displayed no signs of revolutionary fervour, but his charm and wit remained unchanged.

It's a funny old world.

A Policeman Prophet

In November 1948, Princess Elizabeth gave birth to a son, Charles, and English newspapers of diverse political persuasion went overboard with expressions of glutinous sycophancy. My father, who was a staunch Tory-monarchist, surprised me by stating quite boldly that he didn't think Charles would ever sit on the British throne.

Only a month or so before the royal birth, I knew he had refused a request by the League of Empire Loyalists to become a paid-up member. "Don't like the look of them," he said. "Funny bunch."

I think he judged them as only marginally better than Moseley's Union of Fascists. He explained this apparent contradiction in his beliefs by saying that he supported the concept of constitutional monarchy, but thought it unwise to be too fanatical about it.

I found this a bit too subtle for my thirteen-year-old mind to fully comprehend. At school, both preparatory and grammar, we stood for the national anthem and celebrated the sovereign's birthday, and at home had been known to toast the King in brown ale on Christmas Day as a mark of respect. Grandfather, Quartermaster — Sergeant Harry Frank Turner, had been a loyal soldier of Empire and a fervent royalist.

Of course, I now know just what my father meant when he said one shouldn't be too fanatical about the monarchy. Fanaticism was un-British. Foreigners were fanatical and the most fanatical of all were Germans and Frenchmen, both of whom had seen their monarchies collapse. Quiet, staunch respect was what Englishmen should display when supporting their ancient, non-flamboyant and safely dull royal family.

I remember my sister, Mary, asking Dad why he thought the infant Charles would never ascend the throne. He paused and lit a Player's Navy Cut. This of course was a clue that he was struggling to construct an answer that would satisfy both my sister and myself. While I cannot recall his precise words, what followed was a remarkable, condensed précis of the rise and fall of the British Empire and the gradually diminishing role of the crown as he saw it. The general gist of what he said was as follows.

The British Empire once straddled the globe with its dominions and colonies and protectorates but, like all empires throughout history, it was shrinking, collapsing, transforming, reforming, changing. We had just "given away India" in 1947, the year before, so the British sovereign could no longer be king emperor of that vast continent.

As the old Empire evaporated, by agreement or revolution, so would the influence and *raison d'être* of the British monarch. All this, remember, from a Tory-royalist born in 1898 whose whole life, like that of his father, had been spent in the service of this self-same monarchy.

By the time Charles was ready to inherit the crown, decades away, my father believed that the monarchy would have faded and disappeared. But not by revolution or popular dissent, no. Father's view was, in my opinion even today, right on the money. The monarchy would wither and die because people had become indifferent to it. The phrase he used, and this I do remember, was "It will be yawned into oblivion." Half a century later, I see a rehearsal of this trend in the British public's obvious boredom and indifference to politicians of all stripes.

I believe that Dad's prediction about the slow, unspectacular death of the monarchy may still be proved accurate. Maybe not for a decade or so, and certainly not if our present, excellent queen lives as long a life as her extraordinary mother.

But consider this. Can anybody say with hand on heart that if Queen Elizabeth hangs on till she's 95, a perfectly reasonable possibility, that the septuagenarian Prince of Wales and his equally ancient consort Camilla, will ascend to the throne?

Who knows?

And who, by then, will actually care? What a pity.

Colourful Images

One of the great joys of Fulham in the late 1940s and 1950s was the blossoming of outdoor advertising. Great wooden hoardings went up on hitherto abandoned bomb-sites extolling the virtues of Bovril, for example, which, it was claimed, would overcome that "sinking feeling". The vividly coloured poster showed a man in pyjamas, obviously shipwrecked on a vast ocean, sitting astride a giant pot of Bovril.

Another equally colourful example was a massive poster promoting Guinness. It's slogan, which today, like most slogans of those days, would be condemned as politically incorrect in the extreme: "Guinness for Strength". Here a muscular proletarian with sleeves rolled up carried a gigantic iron girder on his shoulder with an air of insouciance. There was often a toucan in the corner of the picture.

Cigarette advertising, reviving itself after the lean war years, was unabashed and forceful. Craven "A", a long-extinct, cork-tipped brand, claimed without a blush, that you should smoke it, "for your throat's sake".

In addition to the contemporary stuff mentioned above, some old pre-war advertisements still remained, particularly in grocers' shops or on brick walls in the

151

Munster Road. These were usually on metal sheets, galvanised and printed in garish colours for Swan Vesta matches, Carter's Little GEC liver pills and Pear's coal tar soap.

Nearly all claimed or hinted that the use of their product would somehow enhance or enrich your health. And of course Robertson's jam used a red-vested, grinning golliwog to promote its particular brand of preserves.

Cinema promotions were also a feature of the outdoor scene. The old Broadway Gardens cinema next to the tube station at Walham Green often showed Tarzan movies starring Johnny Weismuller. One poster I recall depicted Tarzan, naked save for a leather bikini, crouching in a tree top with "Boy", a semi-naked youth with curly hair and rosebud lips. Boy, of course, was Tarzan's son, but today, just imagine what people would make of that image. Incest? Gay sex in the tropics? Writers on the *Guardian* would have a collective, liberal seizure. Or perhaps not. Might be a touch homophobic to object to a big muscular man crouching behind a clean limbed lad with gleaming, hairless thighs.

Generally, the appearance of posters and hoardings added a touch of colour, even glamour, to the drab streets. I loved them; They allowed me to drift into a world of fantasy and aspiration. They also had a long-lasting effect, as 30 years later I was earning my living in the world of television advertising and was, in the 1980s, vicechairman of the British Advertising Association.

152

During the actual war years, I still remember the patriotic posters urging people to "Dig for Victory", i.e. plant allotments, and one warning us avoid "Careless Talk" which was a rather chilling proposition implying that Nazi agents might be listening in to our conversations in pubs and shops. One sticks vividly in my mind. I saw it on the wall of a greasy-spoon cafe in Walham Green. It showed two women in headscarves and overalls drinking tea in what looked like a Lyons Corner House. They were chatting and smoking while at the next table, wearing a mac with the collar turned up, was a man who looked suspiciously like Adolf Hitler, complete with limp quiff and little black moustache. "Careless Talk Cost Lives" was the slogan. Wow! This was something. Two gossiping females, obviously workers in a munitions factory, exchanging information about the calibre and velocity of British shells! And in earshot of the fuhrer! I have no doubt budding feminists of the 1940s era would have bridled at the clear implication that only women engaged in loose talk. The men, I suppose, were either in the armed forces or digging for victory and would have no time for idle chatter.

I only recall seeing one wall poster that had been seriously defaced, although the odd moustache might appear on the occasional hairless female lip. This was for a Pear's soap advertisement which featured a cherubic baby in a tin bath reaching out for a bar of the famous soap which had fallen on the floor. The slogan was, "He won't be happy until he gets it." Some wag had flyposted a picture of a girl in suspender belt and stockings, probably "Jane" of the *Daily Mirror*, over the bar of soap clearly implying that the randy cherub was eager to slake his infantile lust with a fully grown adult female.

I thought it was outrageous, sexy and wonderful.

On the corner of Kelvedon Road where it joined Fulham Road, was a Sunlight Laundry establishment. A metal poster encouraged punters to bring their dirty washing in to have it subjected to the "Sunclean" treatment, a perfectly reasonable proposition you might assume. That is, until a couple of scrofulous yobs stood outside and stuck a sheet of brown paper over the "S", thus exorting people to submit to the "Unclean" treatment. We thought it was hilarious. At least we did until the laundry manager came out and clipped us both round the ears and told us to "piss off".

What fun we rascals had in 1949.

The Dancing Lessons

As soon as I came out of short trousers and into long, grey flannels with turn-ups, my mother announced that I was ready to take dancing lessons.

I was delighted to be rid of the short pants for, at age eleven, I was tall and skinny and my knobbly knees were a source of acute embarrassment. I thought I looked, in common parlance, a total prat.

The prospect of dancing lessons, however, did not fill my heart with vaulting anticipation. Dancing was poncey; girls did it of course, but boys?

My dad couldn't dance. He'd been to dances with Mother in their youth, so he claimed, but he didn't actually dance. He used to sit on the spindly chair at the side of the Salisbury Temperance Hall and watch grumpily while Mother twirled around with various doting swains from the agricultural end of Wiltshire society.

Or so the story went.

Mother insisted that learning to dance was essential and a necessary part of my education process. "You miss out on so much if you can't dance," she insisted, throwing a knife-edged look at father who sat in his police boots in the corner of the room behind a cloud of Player's Navy Cut.

So I was dispatched to sign up for dancing lessons at the Munster Road School where the London County Council provided evening facilities for local people.

On my first visit, mother accompanied me — an insurance policy, no doubt, against my copping out at the last moment.

Munster Road School, five minutes from where we lived, was a typical turn of the century building that was still lit by gas mantles and heated by enormous radiators that clanged and gurgled and pinged and gave off a fierce, suffocating warmth that dried out your throat and made you sweat even in mid-winter.

We joined a queue in the school assembly hall, a long line of weedy boys and girls shuffling over the polished parquet floor. At the far end of the hall, behind a school desk, sat an LCC officer with a big book like a ledger. He was writing down the names of the youngsters who were to join the next "full ballroom dancing course".

My first silent observation was that the LCC officer didn't look as if he were much of a dancer himself. He was about 40, very fat and puce of features and wore a blue serge suit with a waistcoat that strained across his ballooning stomach. Girls outnumbered boys by about three to one, but they didn't look a great deal more enthusiastic than the sullen lads who stared fixedly at their own feet as if ashamed to be there.

At length, we reached the front of the queue and I was committed, in writing, to a full course of lessons.

After the last boy had signed on, the LCC man with the bulging waistcoat, stood up, brushing cigarette ash from his jacket. "This," he said gesturing to his right, "is Miss Holland. She will be your dancing teacher for the whole course."

We all turned and looked and while I cannot speak for any of the other eleven-year-old boys present, I was transfixed, transported even, pierced through the vitals by a Cupid's arrow sharper than a Zulu spear.

Miss Holland was a vision of beauty the like of which I had never experienced in all of my action-packed eleven years. She was about 25 I suppose, small and slim with wavy auburn hair and a tiny elfin face and glasses.

But she had a rosebud mouth, pink and delightful, and teeth so white that they actually gleamed. Standing there in her pale green jumper and skirt with a single strand of pearls hanging over a discreetly swelling bosom, she was, in the words of Oscar Wilde, the complete personification of absolute perfection. Slim legs, tiny ankles like a young fawn and neat little dancing pumps with a strap and a pearl button.

I was in love. No question about it.

There were no lessons on that first day. It was just the signing-on ceremony and I had to wait another week before clapping eyes on the delectable Miss Holland again.

When I did, she was wearing a frock with a pleated skirt, a loose cardigan with long sleeves and the same little dancing pumps. The long-anticipated moment when she would take me in her arms was, however, not to be. Not on the first day at least.

We were each paired off with another partner, mine a pleasant red-haired girl with a gap in her teeth who smelled of peppermint and Pond's cold cream. As the girls far outnumbered the boys, most of them were paired off together. And so the lessons began to the accompaniment of a scratchy Victor Sylvester record played on an enormous brown gramophone in the corner of the hall. We were taught just the three basic dances: the waltz, the foxtrot and the quickstep.

I was a quick student, and by the third lesson, I had grown confident and not a little cheeky. Some of the boys of my age never seemed to conquer the basic essentials and there were scowls and tantrums and even tears from their partners whose toes had been stamped on during the execution of the reverse cross-step in the foxtrot.

Then came the moment, some weeks later, when Miss Holland danced with each of the children in the class, both boys and girls. When it was my turn, I was trembling like a leaf. Being a couple of inches taller than Miss Holland, I had prepared myself for this moment by washing my neck that morning, cleaning my teeth twice. I must have looked, on reflection, like a juvenile Mexican pimp with St. Vitus Dance.

So I took Miss Holland in my arms, my right hand sliding into the small of her back, my left hand holding her little pink fingers at the appropriate angle. Then Victor Sylvester started with a sweeping and fruity combination of brass and strings and we began dancing.

It wasn't an overwhelming success.

It wasn't a disaster either. But I think I must have been clutching her too tightly because she winced a couple of times and when we'd finished, smiled and said, "That was all right Harry, but you mustn't hold me like a boa constrictor."

Talk about punctured lust.

I knew what a boa constrictor was. A snake! Miss Holland thought I was like a snake!

It was at that moment, at the conclusion of my first dance with Miss Holland, that I realised that I didn't really love her after all. When I was inches from her face, I found her eyes were too close together and she must have been wearing a bra constructed of steel mesh that banged against my chest as we danced. And she thought I was a boa constrictor.

I got my certificate though, achieving top marks. Miss Holland was, after all, a very fine dancing teacher.

I took the certificate home. Mother was pleased, but Dad just lit another Player's Navy Cut and blew smoke in the air.

A Pinch Of Salt

Miss Salt lived next door to us in Hestercombe Avenue. She was, I vividly recall, one of the most unusual women I have ever met. In 1946 she was well over 60 years of age, which made her a child of the late 19th century.

Miss Salt was a tiny woman, standing less than five feet, like my mother, but she was a wiry, robust creature with a deeply fissured and leathery skin and piercing black eyes which glittered like small coals under thick black eyebrows. She had never married and was completely illiterate, but she had the personality of Medusa. Her voice was quite remarkable, a ripe, harsh cockney that emerged in a torrent of words that could have pierced steel plate at 50 paces. She lived alone in one room in the house next door and although I must have seen her almost every day during the eighteen years I was at four, Hestercombe Avenue, I never knew what she had done to earn a living, or indeed whether she had any relatives whatsoever.

That she was a Londoner is beyond dispute, but once when I was emboldened to ask her whether she was a native of Fulham, she turned her leathery head towards me and snapped, "Ow do I know? I was a child at the time."

160

This cryptic answer was typical of Salty, who had a reputation for uttering mysterious statements at full throttle while leaning with her elbows on the low wall that separated our two front yards. She had no friends, or at least none that we ever saw.

She existed on spinach soup, biscuits and an extraordinary amount of honey. Yet her energy was prodigious. She would scamper to the corner shops along Waldermar Avenue at a brisk trot clutching a frayed rope basket and wearing a floral print frock, a pullover with moth holes and flat, iron-shod shoes.

In summer, she would spend all day on the front step, or leaning on the wall and she would engage passers by in brief, one-sided conversations delivered in ear-splitting decibels.

She evinced a close interest in my welfare as a young boy. If I emerged from our flat in a shirt and no jacket, she would yell at me, "Catch your death a cold you will!" She would ask my father, as he wheeled his bike out to go to work, if there was "any news?" He even used to pause sometimes and read her selected headlines from the *Daily Express*.

"Aha!" she would shriek at some unusual piece of news. "Serve 'em right."

I don't think she'd ever left Fulham, not even to travel up to the West End. Once, when asked by Salty where I was going, I said "Piccadilly". Her little eyes shone and she sucked her gums in a gesture of contemplation. "Piccadilly," she shouted. "It'll do you no good going up there." Then after a pause, "Where is it?"

She obviously had money coming in from somewhere, probably welfare payments, but whatever it was, it must have been minuscule.

The day I remember most vividly (I was about eleven) was when she waylaid my mother and as we came out of the flat. "Ere!" she shrieked, stopping us in our tracks, "I've been to see the doctor Mrs. T."

What followed was a strange, even bizarre conversation that Harold Pinter or even N.F. Simpson would have devoured hungrily had either of them been present. I remember it vividly, if not verbatim, but the gist of it was as follows:

Mother: "Have you been ill, Salty?"
Miss Salt: (After a pause) "No."
Mother: "Nothing wrong then?"
Miss Salt: (After a longer pause) "He gave me an examination."
Mother: "The doctor?"
Miss Salt: (Even a longer pause) "'E works out of 'is front room you know."
Mother: "His surgery."
Miss Salt: "Front room. Carpets. Curtains."
Mother: "Salty, we've got to be off . . ."
Miss Salt: (Pausing and glancing round to see if anybody might be eavesdropping) "Had a full examination in his front room."
Mother: (Noncommittally) "Ah."
Miss Salt: (After a very long pause) "Naked as the day I was born."
Mother: "Well, I suppose."

Miss Salt: "In his front room. Bare. I was all bare. Know what he said?"

Mother: (Trying to coax me away onto the street) "I've no idea, Salty."

Miss Salt: "He said, 'Ow long haven't you had any down there?"

Mother: (Faintly) "Pardon?"

Miss Salt: "He said, 'How long haven't you had any down there?' That's what he said."

Mother: "What? Where? Look Salty, we've got to . . .

Miss Salt: "I said, 'I've never had any down there, not from the day I was born,' I said. It never grew. Not a bit. Nothing. Never. 'E said, 'I've never seen it before.' That's what he said. Never seen a bare pubic triangle before, in a woman of my age."

This information must have struck my mother like a gong, because she fell silent. Bemused as I was, my eleven-year-old ears picked up the word "pubic" and I knew at once this was a conversation I shouldn't be hearing. "Pubic". A very rude word used by grown-ups instead of dick or fanny. Or so I believed.

Pubic. And Salty, 60 years old, skin like an old cavalry saddle, face like a clenched fist, in her faded floral print frock and irontipped shoes, had no hair on her pubic triangle!!

This was bizarre stuff. Explosive stuff. What would big George Hughes, whose mum had a second-hand furniture shop at Walham Green, say when I told him? What would Sid say? And all the rest of the lads?

Mother propelled me onto the pavement and we walked quickly to the corner of Waldemar Avenue. As we turned into the Avenue, I glanced back at Salty. She was staring after us and chewing one of her boiled sweets that Owen the milkman gave her. She waved a liver-spotted hand and put a finger to her lips.

Clearly the information blurted out concerning her miraculous hairless pubic triangle was classified. My lips would have to be sealed.

By the look on my mother's face, I knew that if I even mentioned it, even to my father, I'd be in some sort of trouble.

Indeed it was never referred to again. Miss Salt had no hair on her pubic triangle and never had. Not even a bristle. She was the human equivalent of a Mexican hairless dog.

It's taken me 55 years to get that off my chest. I feel so much better for having done so.

Rents And Royalty

Most of the houses in Hestercombe Avenue were divided into flats and rented; home ownership in our neck of the woods in 1948 was as rare as central heating.

Landlords, therefore, were the Mr. Bigs in Fulham, the men who turned up to collect the rent in shiny Rover cars or, in some cases, on rickety bicycles with sit-up-and-beg handlebars.

Our landlord at 4 Hestercombe, Mr. Hopkins, was a wry, hollow-cheeked fellow who lived himself in a rented house in Anderson Street in Chelsea. This struck my father as an odd arrangement. Hopkins owned two houses, but didn't live in either of them. He described himself as a builder by trade, but in his neat three-piece suit, black lace-up shoes and Trilby hat, worn always at an angle that was never less than jaunty, he looked more like a music hall comedian or insurance salesman than a horny-handed son of toil.

Short, dapper and thin to the point of emaciation, Mr. Hopkins was a landlord of the shiny Rover-driving class. He would glide up to the pavement outside 4 Hestercombe in his suit and his Trilby and his lace-up shoes and his soft kid driving gloves with the little holes in the back. As he climbed out of the car, he would run a gloved hand over the still warm bonnet as if it were a live horse.

Once, after collecting the rent from my mother and from mad Kate, the park keeper's wife who lived in the flat upstairs, Hopkins let me sit in the front seat of his black Rover. I was deeply impressed. My nostrils flared at the heady essence of leather and warm petroleum fumes. The dashboard was of some kind of burled wood which gleamed like glass and the steering wheel looked enormous, like those I has seen on a number 14 bus.

We assumed, of course, that Hopkins must be a rich man. The car said it all, along with the Trilby hat, gloves and shoes, but the real clincher, for me at least, was the silver nail file which he would withdraw from a leather sheath. He would groom his long, bony fingers with it, concentrating on the operation like a surgeon wielding a scalpel. Those fingers, with their scrupulously buffed nails, had, I determined, spent more time riffling through piles of bank notes than heaving bricks or plastering walls.

But I probably did old Hopkins a disservice. I know now that he wasn't by any stretch of the imagination a wealthy man. We paid £1 10 shillings a week rent and so did mad Kate. He rented a tiny house in Chelsea and no doubt the Rover was his only real luxury.

O.K, there was the suit and the hat at a jaunty angle and the nail file in its little leather sheath. But what the hell, my dad had a Sunday-best suit of similar quality and a Homburg hat and he was only a policeman. Dad once said that Hopkins must have believed that houses weren't for living in, but had to earn their keep.

Hopkins owned two houses in Fulham and both of them, no doubt, had to earn their keep.

Hopkins once asked my father if he wanted to buy 4 Hestercombe Avenue, freehold, for £800! Eight hundred pounds. Or so Dad lead us to believe. Dad refused. Not for him a millstone round the neck, oh no thank you. You paid rent. Once a week. Rain or shine. On the dot. No worries. No responsibilities. That was prudence and stability, 1947 style.

One of the very few houses in Hestercombe that was owner occupied was lived in by a family called Little. Mrs. Little was a plump, square woman of forbidding countenance and her husband, Captain Little, an officer in the British Army.

Now a commissioned officer living in Hestercombe in the 1940s was rare indeed. In fact, unique.

Captain Little however, with his ill-fitting peaked uniform cap and glasses, looked more like an accountant than a warrior. However, the gallant captain had suffered terribly as a prisoner of war of the Japanese and, with typical stoicism, would never discuss his ordeal. He was a modest and silent hero.

The Littles had two daughters, Margaret and Audrey. Margaret was voluble and well read; she borrowed books from my father. But Audrey was a quiet girl who kept herself to herself.

Mrs. Little, she of the forbidding countenance and an austere taste in hats, was nonetheless a kindly woman. It was from her that on those occasions when my mother ran out of, say sugar or sultanas in the midst of frenetic cake-making, emergency supplies were

167

borrowed. Many a cup of fine-grain Tate & Lyle, carried pell-mell 4 Hestercombe, staved off cake holocaust in our tiny kitchen.

But Mrs. Little is remembered largely because she had a sister, Rose, who married into the Clunies-Ross family, a very well to do colonial dynasty who had been granted a lease on one of the Cocos Islands in the Indian Ocean by no less a personage than Queen Victoria.

The original Clunies-Rosses passed this unusual gift down through the generations to Rose's son, John, who became, in effect, a kind of super-colonial landlord on the Cocos island. On the island they grew crops of various kinds, raised livestock and reproduced handsome, coffee-coloured children with wonderful teeth and remarkably cheerful dispositions. John oversaw all this tropical-rural business just as his father and grandfather had done before him. There was no currency on the Cocos, just a form of primitive barter. But it was a tranquil, well-ordered society and inevitably the tabloid press in London got wind of the fact that a young Englishman, John Clunies-Ross, was now a kind of benevolent dictator of an island paradise. They quickly dubbed him "King of the Cocos Islands". John entered into the spirit of this charming illusion and, on his visits to London, even took to wearing a cloak, complete with embossed medallion at the collar and silk lining.

The whole charade, fanned furiously by the press, added a shaft of luminous fantasy to our humdrum lives. When "King" John parked his effulgent, gleaming

Bristol motor car outside the Little's house in Hestercombe Avenue, net curtains twitched and small boys, including me, gaped open mouthed at such displays of opulence.

Only Mr. Hopkins, our landlord, looked downcast, his fine Rover car now relegated to second place next to Clunies-Ross's fabulous Bristol.

The grinding of Hopkin's teeth could be heard two streets away in Burnfoot Avenue, or so my dad said.

The Neckless Wonder

"I'm joining the St. George's Weightlifting Club in Putney," I announced. "It's two and sixpence a visit, but if you're under eighteen, it's a shilling."

"Weightlifting?" said my mother, wiping her hands on her small pinny, "What for? Why weightlifting?"

"To build a massive physique," I said, a shade self-consciously.

My father lit his twentieth Player's Navy Cut of the day and coughed like a horse. I was very skinny at fifteen. Fit and nimble and a school champion sprinter and a member of the first eleven soccer team. But I was like Gandhi, only thinner. Compared to me, Gandhi was obese.

"Look," I said to my mother and showed her a copy of *Health & Strength* magazine. It was full of pictures of young men with huge, rippling muscles and vacant expressions. Their bodies were greased and shone like patent leather. Some of them had bigger breasts than my sister. But they were not called breasts, but pectorals. Or "pecs." I wanted big pecs. And biceps. And long sinewy thighs and a stomach like a washboard.

In actual fact, my interest in bodybuilding had been triggered by accident. I had nipped into a newsagent's and thought I was buying a magazine called *Health & Efficiency*, which was about naturism and was full of naked women playing tennis with their pubic hair blotted out and men whose willies were always hidden by a leaf or a shadow. To be honest, I wanted to look at the naked ladies in the book, but mistakenly asked the newsagent for *Health & Strength*. So instead of a magazine that would be an aid to a fifteen year old's masturbatory fantasies, I had inadvertently acquired the bodybuilder's monthly bible.

Mum looked at the photographs in *Health & Strength* and wrinkled her nose. "Horrible," she said. "Look, he's got no neck." She pointed to a picture of a man with huge trapezius muscles that ran along his shoulders above the collar bone. The ridge of muscle stood up level with his ears, making it look as if his head had been driven into his body by a pile-driver.

But I still joined the St. George's Club and after six months, I had gained a stone in weight and my skinny frame had a light feathering of muscle.

St. George's Club was situated above the Duke's Head pub in Putney and you had to push through the public bar to reach the staircase that led up to the gym which was in the attic. It was always full of men of varying degrees of muscularity all exercising with grim determination on a variety of barbells and pulleys that looked like medieval instruments of torture.

One fellow had an awesome physique. He was called Spencer Churchill and later became a professional wrestler. He had a 49-inch chest and a 28-inch waist. And then there was a tall, blonde man called Georgie

Hughes, whose parents owned a second-hand furniture shop in Walham Green.

Georgie had huge pecs and very wide back muscles called "lats" or latissimus dorsi. "Women love muscles," he said once to me. "They go mad for a good physique. Since I took it up, I can get any girl I want. Easy."

I am bound to say that even when my physique was reasonably well developed and I was in my post-Gandhi phase, the girls were not remotely interested in my "pecs" or my triceps. Even when I wore a white T-shirt two sizes too small, to emphasise my amazing torso. June Wilcox still liked Smudger Smith who was tiny and had no pecs whatsoever. And Pat Pullen was still going out with Peter Pryke who later became a journalist on the *Daily Telegraph*. He played tennis, but he had negligible deltoids and absolutely no trapezius to write home about.

One day at home, after I'd been bodybuilding for about a year, I was posing in front of a mirror in the bedroom I shared with my sister, flexing my budding pecs and making my trapezius stand out, when my mother came in. "I told you," she said, "you've got no neck."

"I'm just flexing my trapezius," I explained.

Mum's mouth went into a thin line. "You've got no neck," she said, in a tone of finality. "All that straining has made your neck disappear."

Dad came in at that moment and summed up the situation in a flash, finally destroying any dreams I might have entertained of becoming a sexually irresistible Don Juan. "No neck," he said, "and look at the spots on his back."

"Acne," said Mum. "All that sweating and straining."

"You can't get a pin between those spots," Dad said.

Why anyone would have wanted to get a pin between my angry adolescent pimples I couldn't imagine. But he was right. I was incredibly spotty.

Right then, I would have swapped my pecs for a nice spot-free back. I've still got good pecs, but the spots have gone and, Mum, bless her, would be pleased to know that in middle age, my neck has finally returned.

An Evening At The Fulham Town Hall

There was a buzz of excitement in the St. George's Bodybuilding Club above the pub in Putney when news reached it that Reg Park, Mr. Universe himself, was to appear in the flesh at the Fulham Town Hall.

Park, a native of Leeds, had overshadowed all of his American rivals like Steve Reeves and snatched the crown for himself.

None of us at St. George's had ever actually seen the legendary Reg, only countless photographs of him in *Health & Strength* magazine and more rarely in an American glossy called *Muscle Power*. We knew his measurements off by heart: chest 52 inches, biceps 19 inches, waist 34 inches, thighs 26 inches, calves 17 1/2 inches. We also knew his dad was a jeweller and that Reg trained five times a week. But to see him. Actually witness this colossus in his awesome posing routine at the Fulham Town Hall was, well, akin to visiting Mars or discovering penicillin.

Tickets for the event were on sale at the club and in a fever of excitement, I borrowed half-a-crown from Doug Wilson, my training partner, and bought my seat in row "G", pretty near the front, as did Doug who was, if anything, a greater fan than I was.

On the great day, a Saturday as I recall, we arrived at Walham Green an hour early on the not-unreasonable assumption that if we were late, our empty seats would be given to some undeserving wretches unable to appreciate the spectacle on offer.

Thus arrived two lads, scarcely sixteen years of age wearing T-shirts a size too small, the better to emphasise their budding adolescent physiques, shirts that had been laundered by their mums and were as white as any soap powder adman could have wished for, and both sporting the proud legend "NABBA" encircled by a kind of Romanesque laurel leaf. NABBA was the proud logo of the National Amateur Body Building Association.

To say the excitement surrounding the Fulham Town Hall on that Saturday afternoon was palpable would be an exaggeration. The crowd shuffling in a queue as the doors opened were calm and vaguely detached. Some were weedy-looking men with fags dangling from the corners of their mouths. Some were women, and women of a dangerously advanced age, probably about 25 or 26. The women were mostly accompanied by male bodybuilders, their status obvious by the tight T-shirts or ridiculously over-padded blue blazers with the NABBA badge on the breast pocket. All the men, even the stick insects among them, affected a rolling gait with arms hanging loosely at their sides as if the sheer weight of muscle, real or imagined, made it difficult to raise them above waist level. This curious

175

walk would, years later, be described by Tom Wolfe in his novel, *Bonfire of the Vanities*, as the pimp roll, although he applied it to tough black kids in New York's Bronx district. It was a walk of slow menace, hinting at explosive strength and panther-like speed should an occasion arise when such a release of energy might be called for.

The Fulham Town Hall was the usual architectural mix of fake imperialism, marble, polished mahogany and tall fluted columns. Inside, attendants of a rat-faced variety in municipal uniforms scanned our tickets with a degree of ferocity not unknown to Nazi Storm troopers when selecting candidates for the firing squad.

Eventually, after our bona-fides had been reluctantly accepted and our tickets not seized as counterfeit, we filed into the large hall in which the promised treat was shortly to shortly take place. As the hall slowly filled, I noticed a strange man in the row in front of Doug and me with hair dyed orange. He wore a velvet jacket of unusual design and smoked a perfumed cigarette from a long holder. As we took our seats, he turned and gave us a death's-head leer.

"Better watch him," Doug whispered, "he's a poof from Kensington."

Now such a description today, apart from being politically incorrect and probably offensive, was, in the opening months of the 1950s, a phrase loaded with significance, caution and streetwise symbolism. That the perfectly harmless fellow in front of us was homosexual may well have been true, but the highly emotive inclusion of the word Kensington was the real clincher. Come on now, cigarette holder, velvet coat and from Kensington! My God, it was only the thin barrier of chairs between us that prevented unspeakable acts of unnatural hideousness being perpetrated on our fine, young, sixteen-year-old, admittedly spotty, bodies.

Before any such outrage could take place however, a man in a tuxedo appeared on stage in front of the curtains and announced that the show was about to commence. The supporting acts, for such they were, consisted of a group of Moroccan tumblers whose nimbleness and athleticism was accompanied by savage cries in some obscure desert language, a bald Negro with more rows of teeth than was necessary who lifted massive weights with his lips and balanced a huge iron globe on the tip of his chin, and a brace of lady jugglers who hurled Indian clubs high into the air while wearing fishnet stockings and curious corset-like bustiers.

Eventually, there being no interval in the delights on offer, the tuxedoed compère appeared once again in front of the wine-coloured stage curtains and, brushing a recalcitrant wisp of hair from his Neanderthal forehead, announced, in a rising falsetto, "Ladeees and Gintlemen, I present tew yew, Mister Universe himself, our own, our very own, Reg Park!!"

And the wine-coloured curtains swept back revealing, mounted on a plinth, the amazing figure of Reg Park. Over six feet tall, his torso oiled and gleaming, Reg Park was indeed amazing. The muscles beneath tanned skin bulged like coconuts. His biceps, larger than a sprinter's thighs, swelled like living things as he flexed his arm. His abdominal muscles, etched and sculpted, resembled a bar of Cadbury's milk chocolate with its symmetrical sections.

Slowly, mighty Reg adopted a series of dramatic poses moving fluently from one to the other, each time displaying more muscles than I thought ever existed in a human body.

His face throughout, displayed no emotion whatsoever, just momentarily falling into a grimace as he performed the "separation of the abdominal wall" manoeuvre which drew gasps from the audience and a low groan of envy from Doug Wilson whose battle to achieve "ripped" stomach muscles himself had been somewhat less than gloriously successful.

Reg's final pose, facing the audience, was Christ-like as he raised both arms and flexed those monumental biceps while simultaneously causing his balloon thighs to tense and quiver like the columns of Samson's temple.

Utterly replete, we clapped until our hands stung and Reg loped back onto the stage to take a bow. Curiously, he looked even bigger than when he was posing — a living monument to what limits the human frame can be driven by assiduous exercise and tolerance of pain.

As we filed into the cold streets of Walham Green, we knew we had witnessed a major event. Silently, we walked towards North End Road, Doug Wilson and I, incongruous in our too-tight T-shirts under the unflattering glare of the sodium street lights. I caught a glimpse of our reflection as we passed the windows of the Times Furnishing Store and the image was sobering. In spite of months of weightlifting at the St. George's Club in Putney, we still looked, compared to the immortal Reg, just like a couple of teenage lads in ill-fitting clothes.

Many years later, I asked myself one question about that memorable evening, and it was this: how did Doug Wilson, my training partner and close chum, know that the man in the velvet jacket at the Fulham Town Hall was a "poof", and a poof from Kensington into the bargain. Maybe we shall never know.

Cannibal Sausages From The Fulham Road

There used to be a butcher's shop in the Fulham Road close to the Munster Road intersection and not a stone's throw from Harold Laski House, the Labour Party's local office. I was sent there once by my mother to buy 2lb of pork sausages. I was about ten years old at the time and this, therefore, was a most sophisticated errand. Clutching a few coins, I entered this awesome place and was struck by an icy blast of refrigerated air. The floor was strewn thick with sawdust and three naked light bulbs flooded the whole shop with a fierce, unrelenting glare.

Two large men in striped aprons stood behind the counter, both wearing straw hats. The younger of the two was serving an old lady with what looked like a slab of liver. He slapped it onto a thin sheet of tissue and then covered it with another. Blood oozed through and he finally rolled it in a sheet from last week's *News of the World*.

The older man was large; not fat, but huge-boned and wideshouldered. He looked exactly as I imagined all butchers ought to look. He had a round, red face with piercing blue eyes and a thick, bushy moustache.

He was chopping an enormous chunk of meat with what at first appeared to be a fireman's axe. The gleaming blade came down with a loud crack as it smashed through bone and cold flesh. I could see the marbling of white fat as the great slab was cleft in two.

He looked down at me from his towering height. "Yes?" he said and his voice rolled slowly over the word like thunder.

"Two pounds of pork sausages," I said.

"Please", he said sternly.

"Sorry. Please," I replied, utterly intimidated.

"Got the money?" he then demanded.

I opened my palm and he poked the coins with a huge knuckled finger. I noticed that the tip was covered in a rather tattered looking bandage or tape. He sniffed and made a wet noise with the back of his throat then raised the axe again to smash into the hunk of meat.

I couldn't take my eyes off his left hand, the one with the bandaged finger. He held the slab of meat steady with it while using his right hand to wield the axe.

Smack! Down came the blade, cutting into the meat an inch away from the bandaged finger. I must have winced because the younger man serving the liver started laughing.

The big man put his axe down and wiped his hands on his bloodstained apron, then he turned to a cold shelf and took down a bunch of sausages, tore one off and placed the rest on a set of big white scales. Satisfied with the weight, he swiftly wrapped the sausages in tissue and the inevitable *News of the World*.

181

I opened my hand, now a touch clammy, and he took the coins. The younger man put his hands on the counter and leant towards me conspiratorially. "Very good bangers," he said. "Dad makes 'em here on the premises." He glanced sideways at the big man, no doubt to conceal a wink. "Always puts bit of his finger in them to add a bit of flavour."

I must have looked poleaxed because they both laughed now.

"Oh yes," said the big man, "it's our speciality. Mind you I can't always do it. I have to wait for the finger to grow back again, like this one." And he thrust the huge bandaged finger at me until it almost touched my nose.

I took my parcel of sausages, and my few coins change, and fled. For some reason, I couldn't tell Mum about the finger when I got home. I just felt that it wouldn't be appropriate. Or maybe I was just scared.

We had the sausages fried that night and I took particular care to chew carefully in case I discovered a piece of fingernail embedded in the meat.

It's a funny thing, but 55 years later, I'm still not absolutely sure that the butcher was actually joking. Oh alright then, I am sure, but wouldn't it be amazing if it had been true? Cannibal sausages from the Fulham Road. Life couldn't get much stranger than that, now could it?

Tea-Time

Nobody in Hestercombe Avenue gave dinner parties. To start with, dinner was what people ate at midday, and the evening meal was usually called tea or, remarkably, the evening meal.

Social entertaining over food was rare, except among relatives, but my mother, ever anxious to broaden our contacts as young adults, regularly provided Sunday tea for as many as half-a-dozen guests: Indian students who had lodgings nearby, a rope salesman (and by that I mean a man who marketed hawsers and twine, clearly a metropolitan sophisticate) and occasionally male dancers from Sadlers Wells whom my sister, in her time in the opera chorus, had befriended.

My father enjoyed these gatherings as they offered him an opportunity to engage in conversations over a wide range of nondomestic subjects. Once, my mother met a Chinaman in the North End Road who appeared lonely. Naturally my mother, a diminutive woman of four feet ten inches, approached him and demanded to know why he looked so gloomy.

"Homesick," he explained. He was about twenty, a law student from Shanghai.

"Then you must come to Sunday tea at our house," was Mother's instant response. And so he did, adding another layer of exotica to our collection of friends.

I found it most illuminating. Brisk conversation over a wide spectrum, led usually by my father, and often quite erudite.

My father, who was remarkably well read, used to let the Indian students borrow books from his book club collection, and they were enthralled to hear of his father's (my grandfather's) exploits in India on the North-West Frontier and later in Zululand.

Tea was served in the back room which overlooked our small garden. A "leaf" was inserted in the big Victorian dining table and covered first with a thick velvety undercloth on which a dainty lace tablecloth would be placed.

Up to six mock Jacobean chairs from Gamages in Holborn, with twisty barley sugar struts and leather seats, would be arranged around the table, supplemented by cane garden chairs. On those occasions when the party grew to ten or more, a wooden plank would be set across two chairs providing a long bench, covered with a blanket and cushions.

Tea was always marvellous. It was amazing how much food my mother could rustle up from her tiny scullery (she never called it a kitchen): mounds of sandwiches on white bread, liberally buttered; Spam, ham, cucumber and cheese, Marmite, raspberry jam and lemon curd. There were also plain slices of buttered bread on which you could spread the delicacy of your choice. Nestle's condensed milk, Bovril, greengage jam, even marmalade.

All at tea-time! And on a police sergeant's wage of less than £6 a week.

Then there were sponge cakes, sugary confections with a pale beige crust; cup-cakes in their corrugated brown paper wrappings; chocolate sponge coated with a hard shell of milk chocolate; doughnuts, the split variety, oozing cream and jam; and after the war, in the late 1940s, big round fruit cakes from Lyons with whole almonds sticking out of their tops next to the crisp burnt currants.

There were also jellies and banana custard and treacle tarts — homemade treacle tarts. But though Mother was a great provider and good cook of plain food, she was the world's worst pastry cook: it would turn out white and hard, like concrete. Many a tooth was chipped by a polite Indian student as he tackled one of Mother's treacle tarts.

But generally it was a cornucopia of food made or bought during the early part of the week.

The guests: the Indians, the Chinese, the rope salesman, the theatricals and my sister's Hungarian boyfriend whom she later married, provided a truly sophisticated salon for a teenage boy eager to learn the ways of the world.

You can't get cup-cakes any more. Not where I live now, at least. Not a lot of people know that.

The Key Flats At
Park Mansions

The only part of Fulham in the late 1940s that could be described as vaguely up-market, was the area alongside Bishop's Park, in particular the Mansion Flats built in 1904, that stretched from the park up to the Fulham Palace Road.

They were spacious and each block had its own forecourt fringed with clipped privet and a scattering of gravel. Some faced the public tennis courts and the tall plane trees that surrounded them.

The men and women who lived in these flats wore smart clothes, suits, hats, polished shoes. I remember seeing a woman emerge from the flats one day wearing a hat with a high brim and a fox-fur slung across her shoulders. The fox tail hung behind her coat and was fastened in the front by the stuffed head of the animal, complete with glass eyes, snout and ears. She wore very high heels and her calf muscles flexed as she walked. Although she must have been about 40, I experienced a stab of lust. In Hank Jansen's books, of which I was a secret devotee, women who wore furs and high heels almost certainly wore suspender-belts and my fevered fifteen-year-old mind immediately conjured a vision of this respectable lady naked except for the fur and the suspender-belt. I was an early convert to such entertaining day-dreams.

One day at the public tennis courts opposite the Mansion Flats, I was passing an idle hour with a few friends. Peter Pryke, who later became a *Daily Telegraph* journalist, was playing tennis, which I shunned as being too posh, while I chatted with the other nonplayers.

One of the boys there that day was called Michael Levene and he lived in the Mansion Flats just across the road. He was well-spoken and neat, with curly black hair and very rosy cheeks. After the tennis match that we were watching finished, I found myself walking back towards Fulham Palace Road with a girl named Cynthia. Tall, spare and very red-haired, Cynthia was sixteen and more than passingly attractive.

It transpired she lived in Doneraile Street, not too far from the park, so I accompanied her to the small terraced house with the stained glass starburst over the front door and she fumbled in her cardigan for a key. I contemplated a lunge. One kiss was all I sought. One kiss on that pretty mouth surrounded by freckles, but she had the key in the door and was halfway in the house before I could put my plan into action. "Bye, Harry," she said, and was gone.

Next day in Bishop's Park, I was with my usual cronies including Michael Levene. Sid, my friend, who was a martyr to acne, asked me outright, "How did you get on with Cynth?"

I knew he fancied her so I decided on the spur of the moment to boast cruelly. "Great," I said. "We necked for half an hour. She's a great kisser." Kissing in 1948 was not like it is today. None of this face-eating, open-mouthed, prehensile-tongue nonsense. "Yes," I continued, embroidering my lie, "I felt her breasts too." A collective "wow" emanated from my audience of fifteen year olds. Sid looked as if he'd been stabbed in the throat. "She let you?" he whimpered. I nodded. The practised voluptuary recalling exotic pleasures. "Yeah. Sure. She loved it."

Then Michael Levene cleared his throat, a very grown up thing to do when seeking attention. "Necked with her for half-an-hour did you?"

"Yes," I blustered. "Half an hour."

Michael Levene frowned. "But I was just a few yards behind you when you walked Cynthia home. I saw you reach her house and leave immediately. I was on my way to Fulham Palace Road."

Caught out in my lie, I think I blustered a little more, but the damage was done. The other lads began to laugh. Sid laughing by far the loudest. I felt utterly humiliated, but the feeling was intensified by the fact that I had brought the humiliation on my own head.

Later that same day, I was at home at Hestercombe Avenue listening, perhaps appropriately, to *Just William* on the radio, when there was a knock at the front door. Mum went to answer it and then called me. "It's a boy for you," she said, wiping her hands on her apron even though they didn't need wiping.

I went to the front door and found Michael Levene standing on the step. "I owe you an apology," he said. "I embarrassed you this afternoon. I'm sorry. I shouldn't have done it."

I was staggered. There was this fifteen year old talking like a wise sophisticate and actually apologising to me, the cocky boaster. I mumbled something along the line of "It's O.K., no problem," and then he turned and left.

When I went back inside, my mother was standing in the hall. "What a well-spoken boy," she said, "What's his name?"

"Michael Levene," I said. "He lives in the Park Mansions."

"Oh yes," replied my mother, "obviously from a good family."

Over tea that day, my mother happened to mention that a well-spoken boy called Michael Levene had called. My father took a bite from his ham and pickle sandwich. "Levene," he said. "Jewish?"

"Yes," said my mother. I was baffled how she should know this. So I asked. "The name, dear" she said, "Levene is a Jewish name." Then to my father, "He lives in the Park Mansions."

"Yes," said my father. "Lots of Jews in Park Mansions. Pots of money."

All this intrigued me. How did my father know that they had pots of money? And why pots? Didn't they have post office accounts like my parents?

"All doing nine-to-five jobs," continued my father, in his mildly anti-Semitic tone. "You never see a Jew doing a pick-and-shovel job."

"He seemed such a nice boy," interjected my mother.

I remained baffled. I thought Michael Levene was more than a nice boy, I thought he was a very sophisticated, grown up sort of person who spoke like the BBC radio announcers.

It was only months later that my sister brought home her first and only boyfriend, the man she was eventually to marry. He was a prefect at Sloane School where I was still a junior. He was a clever, handsome young man called John Forbat, a Jew whose family had fled from Budapest when he was six years old.

My father liked him instantly. So did my mother. "Great family men, the Jews," said my father. "Believe in the family. Clever buggers too. If Mary sticks with him, she'll be alright. You'll never see a Jew doing a pick-and-shovel job."

Poverty And The Single Testicle

Definitions of poverty, along with perceptions of poverty, change from generation to generation.

My parents lived in a small, rented flat, with no central heating, no television, no motor car, an outside toilet; and my sister and I shared a bedroom until she left home to go on the stage at the age of eighteen.

But we were not considered poor. Nor were we. Three hot meals a day, seven days a week. Dad a policeman, never unemployed. We were comfortably off. No foreign holidays, no restaurant meals ever. No pub visits for my parents, they were virtually teetotal. But we were fed and kept warm and cared for.

Poor wasn't like that.

Not in Fulham in 1945.

Poor was like Bill across the road. No Dad. Killed early in the war. Mum was a sickly creature with bad teeth and a rolled-up fag permanently hanging from the corner of the mouth. Six brothers and two sisters, all living in three rooms in a basement flat. Irish. A noisy, cheerful, friendly crew. But poor. Billy, who was the youngest, wore his sister's hand-me-down shoes, horrid little things with a strap and buckle. He had rickets and for a year, his left leg was in irons. His mother used to buy three portions of fish and chips — usually cod — to feed all nine of them. I think it was the one and only meal of the day, except that the kids got school dinners, which helped. His mum couldn't read, but Billy could. He used to borrow books from me and read them aloud to his mum. Enid Blyton mostly.

I went into Billy's flat quite often when I was eleven. It was virtually unfurnished except for lots of beds and mattresses on the floors; lino instead of carpets and sacking tacked up to the windows. It stank of urine and damp laundry and cigarettes. All the children were skinny, with white, pinched faces and big pale blue eyes. They always seemed to have coughs or catarrh or other chesty complaints. His mother had once been pretty, I imagined. She had oval face with the family's huge blue eyes, but now her eyes were sunk into her skull with dark rings under them — a look of perpetual exhaustion.

She died of lung cancer when Billy was thirteen and all the children were taken by relatives in Hammersmith except for Billy, who was a "problem". He'd been in trouble for petty theft from the age of nine and he was sent to a "home" somewhere in North Kensington.

When the landlord, Mr. Austin, from Putney, reclaimed the flat, it was found to be infested with rats and dangerously damp with mildew growing on an inside wall.

I never saw Billy again after he was sent to the home, but for me, forever more, Billy and his mum and his six older brothers and two sisters were the absolute definition of poverty.

Some of the poorer homes in Fulham were still gas lit until 1950. There were streets which had become ghettos for poor Irish families. The streets even had Irish names like Munster Road and Kilmaine Road and Doneraile. Now they house young professionals in the financial services industry, dot-com social climbers and 30-year-old accountants with red faces and pinstriped suits and wives called Lucinda or Arabella.

There is a specific house in Waldemar Avenue, close to where I used to live, that is now so gentrified with its shiny black front door, venetian blinds and trailing geraniums in terracotta pots, that it's hard to believe that in 1948, a man lived there in one of its three flats called Brian the Bollock. No I'm no making this up. I'm only repeating what my father told me.

This particular fellow, a post-office worker, had endured the operation to remove one of his testicles — so it is said, or rather, so my father said. Why both were not removed remains a subject of speculation among Fulham cognoscenti even to this day, but one only was apparently claimed by the surgeon's knife.

The fellow, post-operationally, was henceforth known as Brian the Bollock. Singular, very subtle, very droll. Not a lot of people know that.

Nor indeed wish to.

But it's worth recording, is it not?

Show Time

The Granville Theatre at Walham Green was Fulham's variety theatre. Built in the late 19th century, it had grown shabby after years of neglect during the Second World War, but in the late 1940s, it was home to a kaleidoscope of travelling shows that included jazz bands, magicians, hand-balancing acts and past-their-best opera divas.

The stalls were still furnished with tip-up seats covered in greasy, faded velvet and the carpeting in the aisles was pitted with cigarette burns and part paved with trodden-in chewing gum.

Up in "gods", a smell of dampness assailed the nostrils and on days of heavy rain, small leaks would provide a metronomic drip, drip, drip as accompaniment to whatever act was struggling to entertain on the stage below.

I first visited the Granville Theatre at the age of thirteen with two other boys who were a couple of years older. Being tallish and skinny, I suppose I passed as a sixteen year old as well.

What had drawn us to the theatre was a billboard posted outside a week earlier that advertised the next attraction. It promised in its list of fare, "stupendous Acrobats from Hungary", a "Man Who Would Fill The

Stage with Flags", "a Jazz Trio from Olde New Orleans" and — excitingly — "a cavalcade of Nudes of all Nations". Seats could be purchased on the day in the upper circle, "the gods", for a shilling.

It seemed to three scruffy, acne-pitted and frustratingly libidinous lads that a mere twelve pence to see naked women from all nations was value for money beyond the dreams of avarice.

It was necessary to lie to my parents about my actual planned whereabouts on this particular Saturday, not because they would have disapproved (my sister was already on the stage as a singer touring with Ivor Novello's Dancing Years to the great pride of the family), but to admit that I was going to the Granville to leer over naked women would have made me excruciatingly embarrassed. So the fiction offered to my mother and father was that I was going to play table soccer with friends over near Bishop's Park, a respectable part of Fulham where attractive appartments stood in tree-lined roads close to the River Thames.

Came the agonisingly awaited Saturday and, clutching our silver shillings in sweaty palms, our trio of dangerous sex maniacs headed for Walham Green. The foyer of the theatre was filled with grownups, mostly men, some of whom, I recalled years later in a bout of nostalgic reminiscence, actually wore raincoats. Furthermore, as memory serves, they were dirty raincoats into the bargain. I am convinced that the scornful phrase, "the dirty raincoat brigade", was coined in those heady days of 1948.

Tickets purchased, the three of us scampered up the staircase to the upper circle, the deal being that in the gods you could sit anywhere, so all seats were up for grabs. We dashed down the narrow aisle and settled into three mottled, faintly rickety front row seats. Here you could lean forward and place your elbows on the narrow, greasy parapet which looked over the rest of the theatre and thus secure an uninterrupted view of the stage.

The show commenced, accompanied by a feeble excuse for an orchestra which seemed to consist of sad, balding men in hired dinner jackets. They scraped and blew and twanged their various instruments in preparation for each individual act, except of course for the jazz trio from "Olde New Orleans" who needed no accompaniment.

The Hungarian acrobats were disappointing, except for their moustaches, which were magnificent, and twice the man at the top of a particularly precarious pyramid wobbled and was required to leap off to safety. Had he not done so, we were of the considered opinion that the silly sod would have crashed into the orchestra stalls.

The man who filled the stage with flags was, it transpired, quite fascinating. He came on to a trumpet fanfare and a badly executed roll of drums and then proceeded to FILL THE STAGE WITH FLAGS! Dozens of them. Flag after flag after flag was produced from the folds of his jacket. Red flags, green flags, blue flags, orange flags, flags which were triangular, flags which were square, big flags, medium flags, tiny flags.

He drooped them over a chair, which was his only prop, or just scattered them across the stage or hung them from the half-flats that formed an oblong around him.

A middle-aged man seated directly behind us, whose breath would have felled an ox at 50 paces, remarked to his rain-coated companion in a voice of cynical erudition, "It's all fucking flags."

His friend acknowledged this remarkable observation by replying, "What a way to earn a living!"

The interval followed, planned no doubt to allow stage hands to clear up the flags, a task that would require two men at least five minutes. Or perhaps the man who filled the stage with flags had to clear up his own flags. The answer to this conundrum has never been revealed to me.

As the lights came up, the man with the bad breath lit a cigarette and repeated, with renewed emphasis, his previous mantra about the excess of flags he had just witnessed.

We three also lit cigarettes, but had only two Craven "A" among us. These were passed from hand to hand and lip to lip with a dexterity that would have impressed the man who filled the stage with flags.

After the interval had over-run by at least ten minutes, almost certainly, in the opinion of sewer-breath behind us, because there were "a lot of bleeding flags to pick up", there sounded a particularly long roll of drums and clash of cymbals and the compère, a small man with Brylcreemed hair and a mild speech impediment, announced solemnly that we would now be witness to "a parade of international beauty gathered from the four corners of the world".

A hush fell over the auditorium as the curtains slowly pulled back revealing a darkened stage, the compère standing to one side in front of the drawn back curtain. "Welcome, Miss Poland!" he suddenly yelled and the stage was lit from all sides. On the plinth in the centre of the stage, but well back from the footlights, stood a blonde woman holding an enormous pair of what looked like shields made from white ostrich feathers. Only her face and legs from the knees down were visible. After a few seconds, she lifted the feathered shields and yes, she was naked, one meaty thigh drawn coyly over the other, her pendulous breasts gleaming under the overhead lights. She turned her head and smiled. Then the feathered shields came down again, obscuring the feast of flesh and the lights went out.

That was it. Miss Poland. All ten seconds of her.

"Welcome, Miss France," yelled the compère and this time, when the lights went up, a brunette was occupying the plinth. She wore a beaded cloak which covered her body right down to the ankles. She let the cloak slip, slowly at first, revealing a tiny pair of breasts and then long legs with self-supporting stockings. Technically she was naked. But the man behind us gave a snort of disapproval.

Next came Miss China, a tiny woman whose pose was almost coy. She too wore a cloak which, when cast aside, revealed an ivory-coloured body and, like the rest of the girls, no pubic hair.

And so the parade continued, representatives from the four corners of the world, all naked, all minus pubes, all on the same plinth and all remaining motionless when the moment of disrobing arrived.

A kind of numbness crept over me: not at all what I had hoped would happen. It was a curiously non-erotic display. They were naked, that was beyond doubt but, but, there was something about the whole performance that was the absolute reverse of titillation. Only Miss Brazil, a dusky beauty of about 40, gave any indication of lascivious promise when she licked her lips. Probably just nervous, I thought.

Miss Japan, Miss Ireland, Miss Scotland (a fat redhead with cantaloupe bosoms, who hid herself behind a vast tartan umbrella) and Miss England, a strange lady with a distinct cast in her eye, but rather good legs.

And then the show was over. We three filed out in silence behind the shuffling throng while gorilla-breath continued to mutter incantations about flags and women who ought to be naked but wore stockings and thus cheated the punters of their full treat as promised on the billboards. It was some years later before I actually saw a woman's public hair, but I never again saw a man who could fill the stage with flags.

The Fulham Baths

The Fulham Baths and Washouses were built early in the 20 century at Walham Green. A daunting granite building with a muddy grey façade, it was the place where hundreds of working-class boys and girls in Fulham learnt to swim.

The main pool was housed in a great echoing chamber with white tiled walls and a high domed ceiling. On entering this vast space, one was struck by the overwhelming stench of chlorine that stung the eyes and throat. Here dozens of skinny children in wool bathing suits splashed and floundered under the tuition of lady instructors wearing skull-tight rubber bathing caps. The noise was like bedlam on a bad day: screams, shouts, bellowed orders from the teachers and the magnified roar of splashing water filled this mighty edifice.

I learnt to swim unaided after three lessons, although the first time I took in a mouthful of the tepid, chlorine drenched water, I nearly threw up. My friend Dickie from Parson's Green, was less fortunate. Not only did he throw up spectacularly, showering the surface of the water with that curious combination of bile and tiny fragments of carrot, but he incorrigibly failed to stay afloat. No matter how often the rubber-capped teacher

200

held his legs up and urged him to "kick hard", he just sank like a stone.

After several attempts over several weeks, it was determined that Dickie from Parson's Green would never swim. "He lacks buoyancy," proclaimed a grim-faced teacher.

Some lads from the Lewis Trust Buildings were sent to Fulham Baths by their mums simply to wash. They had no bathrooms at home so a weekly plunge in the pale blue chlorinated sludge was a fair substitute. Some even nicked the slabs of white soap that the Council provided in the toilets so that they could wash their feet and grubby necks in the pool. This was frowned upon by the attendants who would blow sharp blasts on their whistles if they spotted any unacceptable behaviour. "No soap in the pool" was a strict rule, though frequently flouted.

The woollen bathing trunks we had were quite ghastly. They retained water like a sponge and after the vigorous exercise of a swimming lesson, the elastic waistband grew slack and made the trunks droop down almost to your knees. The sight of dozens of bony white children dashing along the tiled area surrounding the pool was like witnessing an invasion of alien mutants with webbed crotches.

In the crowded changing rooms after a swimming lesson, dozens of children tried to dry themselves on the thin cotton towels and many left the premises still damp and clammy. My recollection of all those naked white bodies was vivid. We were all so thin, rib bones showing like xylophones under pale skin, tiny shrivelled penises and scrotums that hadn't yet been filled with falling testicles.

If you stood on one of the slatted wooden benches in the boys' changing room, you could just see through a crack in the wall to the girls' room next door. At eleven and twelve, naked girls looked just like naked boys, minus the shrivelled bit: flat, bony chests, wet hair plastered over their faces, bodies shivering and covered in goose bumps.

One day at the Fulham Baths, a group of young men from the St. George's Bodybuilding Club at Putney came in for a recreational swim. They had the bodies of Greek gods, rippling with muscle. As far as I was concerned, they were another species altogether.

Years later, I joined the St. George's Club myself in order to transform my Gandhi-like physique into something vaguely resembling those suntanned young Adonises.

My parents were very proud when I was awarded my certificate for swimming six lengths unaided. Neither of them could swim, so this was something of a first for the family.

Although I was modestly proficient at the breast stroke, I never mastered the crawl. Something to do with my congenital lack of co-ordination — I couldn't paddle my legs up and down at the same time as I moved my arms in that scooping arc that characterises the crawl.

But, unlike Dickie from Parson's Green, at least I didn't sink.

A Most Unusual Bear

Mrs. Humphreys was a formidable woman who wore blue-tinted glasses and a hair net, not all the time of course, but as far as I could make out, most of the time. She lived across the road from us in Hestercombe Avenue, and her husband Jack, who was a Liverpudlian musician with a small band, seemed unperturbed by her choice of head covering.

She worked in "service" somewhere in Belgravia tending to the vagaries of the rich and when Jack was away on some gig or other, she would visit my mother, uninvited, and engage her in fierce conversations about the price of bacon or coal or how her various ailments had "flared up" again. Because of the tinted glasses, she was affectionately known as Blue-eyes. With her long narrow face and lugubrious expression, she would regale my mother with tales of Carthaginian excess that took place at her employers' house in Belgravia.

As an eleven year old, I only caught snatches of her conversation because when she came to our house, Mother kept her in the hall while I was confined to the back room.

Blue-eyes was voluble. In spades. And she peppered her dialogue with ripe expletives, many of which I adopted in later life. Sentences and even individual words would be spiced by stinging oaths and even blasphemies.

A garment in a shop priced at 50 shillings would be "two pounds bloody ten". Buckingham Palace Road was "Buckingham-sodding-Palace-bloody-Road" and quite neatly, I thought, England's premier holy man was "The Arch-fucking-Bishop-of-bleeding-Canterbury".

Although the conversations with my mother tended to be one sided (monologue is the word that springs to mind) Mother did occasionally get a word in, but her tales of woe of overpriced groceries paled into insignificance beside Blue-eyes's explosions of rhetoric.

One day however, Mother said something that stopped Blue-eyes in her tracks and caused her vermilion-tinted lips to fall open in amazement. The words she uttered were in answer to a question from Blue-eyes as to my whereabouts.

"Where is the boy then?" Blue-eyes had said.

"He's not too well today," replied mother. "He's in bed with Mrs. Bell."

Poleaxed and speechless, Blue-eyes, so Mother recounted later, just stood there with a look of unvarnished horror on her face. Me, an eleven-year-old boy, was in bed with Mrs. Bell, a widowed lady of impeccable credentials from nearby Lalor Street! Even Liverpudlian Jack, the husband musician who was used to the seamy side of life, would be shocked to the marrow when he heard this particular piece of gossip. And from the boy's mother too!

Mrs. Bell, of course, was the teddy bear I cherished, that had been a gift from the woman of the self-same name. For some reason I christened it Mrs. Bell because "Teddy" sounded too ordinary.

So it was true that I was in bed with Mrs. Bell. What would Blue-eyes have thought if she'd learnt that Mrs. Bell had an arm missing and was covered in brown fur and was naked except for a small bowtie.

I slept with Mrs. Bell for many years — just how many I can't remember — but it was my middle teens before she was abandoned. And yet abandoned is not really the right word to describe her demise. She actually disintegrated until all that was left was a long, greasy piece of cloth with no head, arms, legs or fur. I gained great comfort from drawing this piece of rag over my face as I fell asleep.

Mrs. Bell was irreplaceable and I never owned another teddy in my childhood, although now I have a dozen or so, kept, of course, for the grandchildren when they visit.

None of them is called Mrs. Bell.

Or even Blue-eyes.

Just as well really; psychiatrists would have a field day with me if any of them were.

Fog

In the late 1940s and early 1950s, London still suffered its traditional "pea-souper" fogs that enrobed the city in a yellowish, acrid blanket for days on end. November was the month when this mixture of damp air and industrial emissions struck most virulently.

The tabloid papers were full of startling tales of asthmatic pensioners and other frail members of the public collapsing in the street as they inhaled the deadly toxins.

We still burnt coal fires at home, belching out our own share of grey smoke that mingled with the coke fumes of the local gas board and the powerful stench of the great lorries as they trundled through the streets on their vital errands.

The politicians were still rabbiting on about clean air legislation and doing absolutely nothing about it. Many people, young and old, dreaded the arrival of the November pea-soupers; they restricted movement, aggravated those with bronchial complaints and usually heralded an increase in street crime, burglaries, muggings and handbag snatching.

Fulham, being so close to the River Thames, used to endure fogs of prodigious intensity. A rich, swirling, caustic cloak would slide through the streets, knee-high at first, but rising like a huge smoky tide until it obscured everything more than a few feet away. The street lights would struggle to penetrate the near Stygian gloom, giving off a feeble, watery glow that was dissipated within mere yards.

But I loved the fog. So did most of my scrofulous young companions in Fulham. Fog meant mystery, drama, excitement. Street games took on an eerie, even dangerous, quality.

At eleven years old, I had read tales of Jack the Ripper that evoked the London of early Victorian times — cloaked figures moving silently through cobbled streets on missions too awful to contemplate. And of course fog. Lots of fog.

Playing in the streets near Hestercombe Avenue, where we lived, was particularly thrilling during foggy days. People, buildings and other objects became unfamiliar, alien things that could only be identified when you actually stumbled across them. Houses loomed at you through the fog. You experienced the thrill of being lost in a road or alley that days earlier might have been as familiar as the back of your hand. Shadowy figures loped past you, close enough to touch or even smell but, with collars turned up and hat brims pulled down, they defied identification.

And people behaved differently in the fog. Certainly we did. We became more daring, more devil-may-care. I remember kissing Helen Searle, aged eleven, with an intensity that shocked us both as we stood on her fog-bound doorstep in Ringmer Avenue. Why? I'll never know precisely. But I'm sure the fog had something to do with it. Perhaps because it masked one's movements from prying eyes, or maybe, possibly, subconsciously we thought fog was the first trump of doom, a smoky signal of approaching Armaggedon and we should snatch at our pleasures before oblivion engulfed us.

My father still cycled to work with a mac covering his policeman's uniform and his helmet concealed in his saddle bags — on foggy days, he cycled very slowly and when he was on his way home, after night duty, my sister and I would stand on the step at the front door of 4 Hestercombe Avenue and peer into the gloom to watch for the first feeble glow of his bike's front lamp as he approached the house.

The really bad days were when the fog appeared suddenly, moving swiftly from the Thames and the heights of Putney Common to grasp Fulham like a cold glove.

One late November afternoon which had commenced with clear skies and insipid sunshine, a group of us were in Bishop's Park playing football on the tarmac which surrounded the old Victorian bandstand. Suddenly, through the trees and the municipally planted shrubs, a rolling fog manifested itself. It came off the Thames and within minutes we were totally surrounded by the stuff. The game, which in any case was of an exquisitely informal nature, was hastily abandoned and we all dispersed to find our way home. I remember clinging close to the park railings to keep my bearings and being surprised how long it took to reach the Fulham Palace Road.

208

The next day, when the fog had thinned a little, I sped to my various friends' houses to ascertain that they too had reached the sanctuary of their homes the night before. Nobody had telephones, so the waiting was particularly poignant. To my utter disappointment, not one of my chums had met with any kind of disaster or adventure whatsoever. No masked figure in a cloak had accosted them. No slavering Alsatian had loomed out of an alleyway to tear them limb from limb. At least one of them could have made up a story, I thought, some dreadful incident that could be recounted again and again over a strawberry milkshake at the Black and White milk bar. Not enough imagination among those lads I fear. It was probably then, at scarcely eleven, that I first realised that the quality of a good anecdote was not whether it was true — how awfully tame — but whether it was entertaining. Absolute veracity was not the vital ingredient.

And fog, I also concluded, was the spur to imagination. Standing in that billowing, silent cloud of grey and yellow where no shape could be seen clearly, all you had was what you imagined lay around the next corner. It's probably a pretty poor show to admit it now, but when all is said and done, I rather miss the old London fogs. November in Fulham will never be quite the same without them.

The Boys From Walham Green

The Walham Green Boys were feared throughout Fulham. Their notoriety spread from the North End Road towards Earls Court and back again beyond Hammersmith. Today, they'd be called muggers. In 1949, they were called yobs. They were mostly very young; fifteen or sixteen years of age was probably the average for the gang. They wore crêpe-soled shoes and narrow, drainpipe trousers, string ties and shirts with long pointed collars. Most of the time they remained dormant, lounging in knots of six or seven on street corners, under lampposts or outside Black and White milk bars.

They were exclusively white boys; the great West Indian immigration was still some time in the future. Skinny, pasty-faced, pimpled and blemished, they all seemed to have perfected the sullen, feral gaze of the hardened street hoodlum. They lived in the tenement blocks liked the Lewis Trust Buildings in Fulham, although some came from Chelsea or Putney to associate with the notorious "Green Boys".

It was a loose kind of association where bored and idle young men with a penchant for petty violence could mingle with others of a like mind. Their occasional outbursts of violence weren't fuelled by alcohol as most of them were too young to be allowed inside a pub. They became active on a Saturday afternoon, particularly when Fulham FC were playing at home at Craven Cottage. They were, it could be said, the ancestors of our current football hooligans. Hunting in packs, they would pick on a lone boy or two who perhaps attracted their attention by dressing differently, that is in a vaguely middle-class kind of way.

A blazer and grey slacks were not the things to be wearing if you were walking alone down the Fulham Road at five o'clock on a Saturday afternoon. I know this because I once became a target of the Green Boys on the day Fulham had lost 2–0 to Blackpool in a cup-tie at the Cottage.

I'd watched in open-mouthed awe from the front of the terraces as the great Stanley Matthews mesmerised the Fulham defence. His ball control and speed over short distances was little short of phenomenal. Time and time again, weaving and swerving past the outstretched legs of Joe Bacuzzi and Harry Freeman, the Fulham full backs, Mathews would send his cross curving into the Fulham goalmouth as if it were a guided missile.

As the final whistle sounded and Fulham conceded defeat, I filed out of the ground in my new grey long trousers and over-large blue blazer with the Sloane School badge on the breast pocket. This was a gold and black shield of the Cadogan Arms as Sloane School lay within the great swathe of London owned by the Cadogan Estate.

Once outside the ground, I cut into Harboard Street and started loping towards Fulham Palace Road, when I was suddenly aware of a group of four or five boys very close on my heels. The Green Boys. Of this I had no doubt. One glance was enough to confirm the fact - thin, bony faces pitted with acne, long jackets, suede shoes with two inch crêpe soles and the sinister cracking of knuckles, a speciality of which the Green Boys were inordinately proud.

I knew what lay in store unless I could reach the safety of the busy Fulham Palace Road. A week earlier, my friend August Kratz, a Spaniard living in the next street to us in Hestercome Avenue, had been walking along Munster Road on a Friday evening and, just as he passed the Munster Road Secondary Modern, a group of five lads had rushed directly at him from Colehill Lane and in spite of his taking evasive action, they had trapped him by Ringmer Avenue and given him a beating. Punches and kicks were rained down on his head and body leaving him bruised and shaken. Completely unprovoked, and executed with the fierce efficiency of a pack of wild dogs, it was a classic Green Boys assault. Later, August Kratz said he thought he had been attacked because he "looked" at the gang. Shades of Robert de Niro in his "Punk" mode gazing at his own reflection in a mirror and mouthing the evergreen tough-guy question, "Are you looking" at me?"

Looking at the Green Boys was clearly a mark of disrespect. You were "dissing" them, in modern parlance, and just looking was like touching a detonator.

However, as I proceeded at an increased pace along Harboard Street, my followers started shouting the usual slogans. References to my grey slacks and blazer were salted with pseudo-sexual epithets: "Hey prick-face, where'd you get those trousers?", "Oi cunt, your bleeding coat's too big."

Then I felt a missile strike my back, just below my left shoulder blade. Later I discovered it to be a hardened dog turd. Then I started sprinting. Now, at fourteen, I was already a fast runner, junior champion at Sloane School, so I just let it rip, fuelled by fear of course, and I kept sprinting till I reached the bustling sanctuary of the Fulham Palace Road with its trolley buses and pedestrians and men on bikes.

I turned, breathless, to see how close my would-be tormenters were, but they'd given up the chase and were no longer in view.

Four years later, when I was called up to do my National Service, I was posted to the Royal Artillery barracks in Oswestry. In my barrack room on the first night, I met a lad who came from Fulham, a roughly spoken lad who seemed to have a lot of trouble getting his kit in order and consequently incurred the wrath of the lance-bombardier in charge of our hut. We became friends, in a mild, off — hand sort of way. He later told me he'd been a "Green Boy", admitting that he'd often been involved in violence and unprovoked intimidations in Fulham. He went on to become a regular soldier, and a very good one indeed. I believe he finally made the rank of battery sergeant major.

So many of those young yobs, or hooligans, in the late 1940s and 1950s went into the armed services to do national service and found that their penchant for violence and excitement, when properly disciplined and channelled, made them exceptionally good servicemen.

A hundred and thirty five years earlier, the Duke of Wellington had summed up this curious situation in two of his most famous quotes. Of the common soldier, he said: "They are the scum of the earth," but then added later, "Look what fine fellows we've made of them."

The Ubiquitous Mohammed

Although Fulham was a staunchly Labour stronghold and usually returned a Labour member of parliament with a substantial majority, other political parties managed to survive and even prosper.

All three main parties had youth sections. The Tories had their Young Conservatives, Labour their Labour League of Youth and the Liberals — well, then as now, it was something so vague and boring that I cannot for the life of me remember what it was called. The No-Hopers perhaps, or even Gladstone's Rump.

However, I do remember a curious incident in my late teens that still causes me to smile when I recall it, as I frequently do. What happened was this. I joined the Fulham Young Conservatives, Dad being such a dyed-in-the-wool Tory that any other course would have been regarded as high treason. We were a small but motley crew who tried, unsuccessfully, to mimic the social behaviour and leisure activities of the infinitely more affluent Young Conservative groups in places like Esher and Putney. Of politics, we knew little and even that was based on tribal instinct and parental decree.

Dad, although a true blue, was never an extremist. I once attended a meeting of Sir Oswald Mosley's fascist group in a spirit of curiosity more than anything else and when I told my father, he was apoplectic. "Wicked, evil enemies of Britain and freedom," was how he described Mosley and his unsavoury gang.

The problem with Fulham Conservative Party was membership, both getting and retaining it among a population which was almost entirely working class. But they didn't do too badly. The youth section was wooed with dances at the church hall, table tennis, river trips to Richmond and other delights. I found it excruciatingly boring.

One day we did, however, recruit a young Asian boy called Mohammed, a delightful lad who had moved into the area with his bus conductor father, also Asian, and his English mother. There was great excitement among the grandees of the Fulham Conservative Party when it was announced that we had signed up Mohammed.

He came to meetings, made friends easily, danced well, beat most of us at table tennis and was generally a popular and delightful fellow.

One Saturday morning, I was in the North End Road shopping with Mother, a duty I found even more stultifyingly boring than a Tory whist drive, when an open-backed Ford van appeared weaving a serpentine path between the stalls and barrows. On its sides were plastered Labour Party posters and a large photograph of Clem Attlee, the Labour prime minister, was fixed to its front radiator.

Seated in the back was young Mohammed in a dark green duffel coat with a woolly hat. Pinned to his coat was a red rosette, the scarlet symbol of socialism!

216

It was a couple of days before I saw Mohammed again, this time outside Frost's the grocer in Fulham Road. I accosted him and demanded to know how he could be so cynical to leave the Conservative Party without telling anybody and then join Labour.

Mohammed gave me one of his winsome smiles. "Oh, I haven't left the Conservatives, Harry. I just joined Labour as well. They have billiards on Tuesdays."

"You've joined Labour as well?" I parroted.

"Yes, why not?" he said. "And I'm joining the Liberals too."

And so he did, treating each of the three political parties' youth sections as social clubs.

I can't remember what happened to Mohammed in the long run. His membership of the Young Conservatives did lapse eventually, but it is quite possible that he retained membership of the other two.

In moods of introspective reflection, I often wonder if Mohammed also joined the Communist Party, the League of Empire Loyalists, the National Union of Fascists, the Salvation Army and the Flat Earth Society as well.

Probably not. None of the above had youth sections and I doubt if any of them had billiards on Tuesdays either.

Money

Although money was in short supply in our household at Hestercombe Avenue, the small policeman's wage my father brought home was at least regular and secure. He was paid in cash, weekly, a few pound notes and coins sealed inside a tiny brown envelope.

Mother, as Chancellor of the Exchequer, Treasurer and General Finance Director, controlled the household budget with imagination, prudence and dexterity.

Pay day was a Friday, and if father was on traffic duty at Hyde Park Corner, mother would travel up on the 14 bus from Fulham to retrieve the unopened pay packet from his tunic. It was a fascinating ritual which I observed on more than one occasion as a small boy.

Father would be standing in the middle of Hyde Park Corner wearing white gauntlets and directing traffic. Mother, in her "going up West" hat, a tiny taffeta job with a feather (Gamages, 3/6d) would scurry across the road from the pavement outside St. George's Hospital (now the Lanesborough Hotel) and plunge her gloved hand into his tunic to extract the pay packet.

Many a cab driver's mouth fell open as he chugged around Hyde Park Corner and observed a tiny woman in a mauve coat and feathered hat mugging a tall policeman while he was on duty.

The ritual was of course performed with Dad's agreement. Pay day coincided with the day that many weekly bills had to be settled and Mother was a stickler for paying things on time.

One of the most vivid images of my childhood was of my mother, weaving between the Sunbeam Talbots, Alvises and Ford Populars at Hyde Park Corner, blithely ignoring the angry hoots of drivers as she skipped through gaps in the traffic to reach her goal: the towering, helmeted, moustachioed figure of my father in his gleaming boots and dazzling white gauntlets.

I would watch this display of nimbleness and pluck from the safety of the pavement, marvelling at how my mother always emerged unscathed from the operation, the brown pay envelope firmly tucked into her blue handbag. Mission completed, we would board the 14 bus and head back to Fulham.

I often wondered what would have happened if a passing police inspector had spotted the pay packet ritual. Dad surely would have been in breach of police discipline, or worse, Mum could have been arrested.

"No chance of that happening," Dad once explained when I raised it with him. "The Duke of Wellington keeps an eye on me. He'd tip me off if any police brass was in the vicinity."

The Duke of Wellington's statue, resplendent on his charger, Copenhagen, dominated part of Hyde Park Corner and his bronze gaze covered the whole area. Silly me. Why the hell did I ask such a dumb question?

219

After my mother had returned home and opened Father's pay packet, she would put half a crown into the "rent" jar on the mantelpiece and another 2/6d in the "doctor's" jar. Shilling pieces were kept in a tin at the top of the cellar stairs specifically to feed the eletricity and gas meters which were housed in the cellar on the wall above the piles of nutty slack and chopped firewood.

My pocket money was about half a crown a week, but I would have to ask for extra contributions if I wanted to go to the cinema. Occasionally, these requests were refused and it was after one such refusal that I embarked on my first act of criminality.

At age eleven, I had a varied collection of friends, some from our road, Hestercombe, others who hailed from the dodgy end of the borough, like Walham Green. These lads were streetwise, tough, feral and to me at least, awesomely heroic. They showed me how four boys could get into the Red Hall Cinema at Walham Green for the price of one.

The manoeuvre was simplicity itself, provided you knew the exact lay-out of the cinema. One of us, often the eldest, would gain entry quite legitimately by paying his one and threepence at the cash desk. Once inside, and shown to his seat by an usherette with a torch, he would slip out to the gents' toilet, an area with which he had made himself familiar, and open one of the windows. This particular window, carefully chosen, opened out onto a narrow alleyway that ran alongside the cinema. The remaining three of us who made up this larcenous quartet, would be loitering in the alley and, with an agility seldom observed outside the monkey house at London Zoo, we would wriggle through the narrow space and into the gents' loo. The boy who had earlier obtained entry by legal means, stood sentinel by the urinals as we three dropped in.

Then, with a casual insouciance bordering on the sublime, we would saunter into the theatre and choose our seats. The technique was 100% successful provided we chose a matinee performance, when the cinema was scarcely ever more than a third full.

Once, on an occasion I recall with burning humiliation, we attempted the operation on a Friday evening during the playing of a Tarzan movie. Getting in was no problem at all, but as we swaggered into the main auditorium from the gents' toilet, we were confronted with a packed house. Not a free seat to be had. An usherette built like a concrete gun emplacement and with a face like ten pounds of condemned pork, challenged us with a flourish of her torch. "You've bunked in," she hissed. And we had, bunking in being the technical phrase to describe illegal entry.

Caught thus, bang to rights, we had no alternative save retreat, and this we executed with dispatch, exiting through the lavatory window of the gents' pursued by the usherette, a clear toady of management who uttered threats of arrest, exposure, punishment and a clip round the ear with her torch.

Bunking in had to be abandoned when we reached the age of twelve, not because of any developing sense of civic responsibility, but because we'd grown too big to squeeze through the gents' toilet window at the Red

Hall Cinema at Walham Green. Mother nature had taken a hand and probably saved us all from becoming cat burglars for life.

My father, the policeman, knew nothing of my life of crime, and indeed I only confessed it to him long after he'd retired from the police. His reaction was one of magisterial disdain. "You were just a child," he said, puffing on his thirteenth Player's Navy Cut of the day. "You did wrong of course, but," here he paused and exhaled a long plume of smoke, "you were too young to appreciate criminal responsibility." Thanks Dad.

But thanks also to Providence. Just imagine how embarrassing it would have been for a police sergeant's son to be nicked for breaking and entering. And at Walham Green, Fulham's roughest neck of the neighbourhood.

Fifty years later, I was tempted to reprise my illegal entry techniques while queuing outside a basement jazz club in New York, but alas, I could detect no gents' lavatory window leading into the adjoining alley and I had no companions with me anyway. Apart from which, had there been such a window, it might have led into the ladies' loo and the consequences of dropping in on a bunch of right-on-hippy females with their knickers round their ankles would have been more than flesh and blood could stand.

Ten Oncers In The Hand

The man with the pock-marked cheeks and the bouffant hairstyle snapped open his wallet. "Every week, ten oncers — in the hand," he said with great emphasis on the last three words. "In the hand, boy."

I was impressed, but then at fifteen I was, I suppose, very easily impressed.

The wallet being held up for my inspection was of the finest lizard-skin. Or so the man with the pock-marked cheeks and bouffant hairstyle insisted. "The finest," he repeated, fixing me with his watery blue eyes.

Then he pulled a wedge of bank notes from the wallet of finest lizard-skin and splayed them like a deck of cards. "Ten oncers," he said, by way of explanation.

And indeed I could see with my eyes the ten crisp one pound notes fanned out in his huge pink palm. His name was David, or Dave as he preferred to be called, and he was a master bricklayer in Fulham. Just what the difference was between an ordinary bricklayer and a master bricklayer was too subtle for my adolescent brain to grasp, so I nodded cravenly at this piece of information when Dave offered it to me.

"Yes," he said, almost to himself, "Work my bollocks off all week. Earn the dosh. In the hand mind you. In the hand. Every Saturday morning. Like clockwork. Ten oncers and that's not all."

He paused and wiped a fleck of foam from the corner of his mouth. "No boy, that is not all."

Naturally, I marvelled at what more could be revealed by Dave. After all, ten oncers in the hand on a Saturday after working your bollocks off and a wallet of the finest lizard-skin. What else could there possibly be?

Dave gave a roguish smile, amused no doubt at my childish innocence. "Keep a few quid back just in case. On top of the wages. Do you follow me?"

Baffled, I nodded meekly. Before my grovelling hypocrisy could be exposed, Dave continued his monologue in a fruity, cockney baritone. "Yes. Cop of load of this," he said, holding out the wallet of finest lizard-skin. Peeking out from the folds of the wallet were three white pieces of paper. At first I thought they were letters. Then Dave eased them free and held them between his thumb and forefinger. They were uncreased five pound notes. Absolutely beautiful. "Go on," said Dave, "touch 'em."

I reached out and put my finger on the three big bank notes. They "crackled" as I touched them, but I think Dave had manipulated them to make them seem alive. "Emergency supplies," smirked Dave, "case I get lucky." Then he turned away from me and addressed his next remarks to a knot of four or five other boys who were a little older than I was. We were all standing on the towpath at Putney looking across the Thames to Bishop's Park in Fulham.

"Get yourself a trade," he said. "Don't fuck about. Get a trade."

One of the boys I knew called Sid, who had more pock-marks than Dave plus some still active pimples, shrugged non-committally. I knew he wanted to get a job in an office in Piccadilly for British European Airways. A clerical job.

"Look," said Dave patiently, "you don't want to ponce about in an office, clerking." He said "clerking" as if it were a contagious disease of unparalleled hideousness. "Get a trade. Look boy, I'm my own man, know what I mean. Work hard all week, then of a Saturday night, I'm away. See this whistle?" He pointed at his suit (his whistle and flute). Cecil Gee's this whistle came from. Fourteen quid. Gabardine."

It was a fine suit, with wide padded shoulders and a long draped jacket, tight trousers with a raised seam down the sides and navy blue shoes to complete the ensemble. Dave certainly looked like a man who could comfortably be "away" on a Saturday night although I only had a vague idea of what it meant. His hair was straw blonde and piled high off his forehead. It glistened with Brylcreem and the sideboards were razored to perfection halfway down his cheeks. He looked the complete sartorial dandy, his white waxy face set off nicely by the silver-grey gabardine suit from Cecil Gee's of Shaftesbury Avenue, Piccadilly.

The only clue to his occupation was the big red hands that hung like sides of beef from the cuffs of his suit. The nails were bitten stumps and the fingers scored with tiny scratches and abrasions. Huge white

225

knuckles bulged under the skin like subterranean onions. Dave was eighteen years old. I thought he was magnificent.

It was only later that I learnt that he wasn't a master bricklayer, or even a bricklayer. He was an unskilled labourer who aspired to be a master bricklayer.

But hey! He had a suit from Cecil Gee's and a wallet of finest lizard-skin full of pound notes and crisp white fivers. He also confidently expected to get lucky on a Saturday night. A charmed life? Or what?

I had no career plans and the prospect of work in an office filled me with a lurking dread. Maybe I'd be a policeman like my father. Excitement, uniform, arresting people? No, that didn't sound too good either. However, theatre or journalism seemed vaguely attractive.

I now confess that in spite of my progress at Sloane School and my membership of both the school Shakespeare Society and the Fulham Library, I seriously contemplated, that day on the towpath, joining big Dave in the building trade.

I'm glad the moment passed because some months later, I heard that Dave had been out of work for six weeks and according to my friend, Sid, he hadn't been seen at the Hammersmith Palais in his gabardine suit for simply ages.

A Question Of Colour

I encountered my first example of racial prejudice in Bishop's Park in 1948. Looking back on the incident in the new millennium, I am more than ever convinced that race hate is an acquired condition. Children are totally without it. Sadly, they learn it from the grownups and at a disturbingly young age.

I was playing football, improvised football, on the great stretch of tarmac that surrounded the Bishop's Park Victorian bandstand. Four coats, strategically placed, provided goal posts and what we kicked around was a nearly bald tennis ball. Ten lads, all about thirteen years of age, stripped to the waist and running around like dervishes. On our side was a boy called Samuels — Sam for short. He was black or, to be more precise, the colour of milk chocolate. He was an absolute natural: fast, lithe and amazingly skilful with the ball. His parents, who had lived in Fulham for 30 years, originally came from Sierra Leone.

As we played our frenzied version of five-a-side soccer, a small knot of strollers paused to watch. One was a man of about 25 who was wearing one of those long leather overcoats with lapels which you saw in war movies. Suddenly he yelled out, "coon" and then doubled up with laughter.

None of us had the slightest idea that the word was shouted as an insult.

"Coon" he yelled again. Even Samuels ignored it and we played on.

The park keeper, Mr. Bailey, who lived in the flat above my parents in Hestercombe Avenue, suddenly came loping across the tarmac carrying his pointed stick. At first we thought he was going to reprimand us for having no shirts on. Park by-laws prohibited the exposure of flesh in the bandstand area. But Mr. Bailey wasn't about to admonish us for our semi-nudity. Instead, we saw him approach the man in the leather overcoat and words were exchanged.

At this point, the game stopped. Voices were raised and leather jacket adopted a threatening posture. Then Mr. Bailey prodded him in the chest with the blunt end of the stick and the man turned and walked away. When he reached the edge of the tarmac, he turned again and shouted "nigger" before scurrying out of view. Now we all knew that the word was not intended as anything but an insult.

Samuels shrugged and seemed unconcerned. Mr. Bailey came over and said in his soft Geordie drawl, "Shirts on, lads," then to Samuels, who was bouncing the tennis ball up and down with the palm of his hand, "Where are you from, lad?"

Samuels looked blank.

"Where do you come from?" repeated Mr. Bailey.

"Kilmaine Road," said Samuels.

Mr. Bailey laughed, a curious almost silent laugh. "No, where was you born lad?" Bailey insisted.

Another blank look from Samuels. "Battersea," he said, "Why?"

Bailey laughed again. Not harshly, for he was a kindly, large sort of man with a slow, avuncular manner. "Well now, that bloke in the leather coat told me to tell you, lad, to go back to where you came from."

Samuels frowned. "What, Battersea?"

More laughter from Mr. Bailey. "He didn't think you was from Battersea. He thought you was from somewhere else."

This struck us all as not only mysterious, but completely pointless. Why should a complete stranger be interested in where we lived.

We donned our shirts over sweaty bodies, and continued our game.

When it was over — we lost 48–12 or something equally ludicrous — we all forked out threepence and bought ice-cream cornets from Maria who kept a barrow outside the park gates.

Before we broke up to go home, Samuels nudged me in the ribs. "I know where that bloke thought I came from," he said thoughtfully.

"Where?" I said.

Samuels took a big lick of ice cream. "Bleeding India," he said.

Later at home I thought about this. Samuels couldn't have come from India. Indians were supposed to be red. Sam was brown.

It was all very confusing.

Real Football

At age ten, before I went to Sloane School in Chelsea, which had its own sports ground at Roehampton, my soccer playing was confined either to the hard asphalt playground of Sherbrooke Road Primary or the equally hard, but more spacious area around the bandstand in Bishop's Park.

A certain amount of improvisation was necessary and the ancient rules of association football were stretched to breaking point. The number of players on each side was therefore flexible. I've played with six-a-side and sixteen-a-side. The ball was always a tennis ball which had lost its fluff and was regularly replaced by nicking stray ones that had been struck outside of the tennis courts by over-exuberant players up by the Park Mansions.

Goal posts were coats or discarded shirts. The length of the pitch was variable. There were no discernible touchlines, the ball could be bounced off low walls around the flower beds and still be in play. Only if it fell into the clumps of hydrangeas or roses was a "throw-in" permitted.

The game was fast, played at a cracking pace by skinny ten year olds in sandals or plimsoles. I developed an amazing skill at dribbling a bald tennis ball past a forest of bony legs and scoring a staggering number of goals.

This was partly possible because of the absence of a cross bar. No shot was ever too high to be discounted provided it passed between the crumpled coats that served to frame the goalmouth

Occasionally, in the middle of a furious game, with the score at something like 46–22, a woman would wander across our pitch pushing a child in a pram. Play would stop, but once the ball dropped into a pram, the woman protested, and the park keeper, Mr. Bailey, who lived above my parents' flat in Hestercombe Avenue, drove all 37 of us off the pitch waving his pointed stick which was normally used for picking up leaves.

After a suitable lapse, we would re-assemble and play would continue.

Mr. Bailey turned a blind eye to this. It was an unspoken agreement between us that he would drive us from our game with whips and scorpions if necessary when a passer by — usually an old person or a mother with pram or pushchair — made a complaint.

Once that person had moved on, we would re-appear from behind the bandstand where sanctuary had been sought and replace the cloth goal post, produce the greasy tennis ball and continue the game.

Then one day, when I was eleven or just shy of it, we moved our game to an area called the Moat Gardens. This was basically a large field, screened by trees and railings that ran parallel the Fulham Palace Road and had once been to part of the grounds of the Bishop of London's Palace. We believed, and still do, that it was called the Moat Gardens because originally a moat had surrounded the palace in the distant mists of the past.

As the gardens consisted of rough meadow grass, a bald tennis ball would not have been suitable and one of our number produced a proper football, leather and ominously heavy with thick lacing.

Coats still provided the goal posts except when we were about 27-a-side and two widely spaced trees were used at one end of the pitch. On these occasions, two goalies were allowed as the gap between these "posts" was about double that of a standard goalmouth.

We played hard and fast as usual. Body contact was obligatory and we developed a cunning technique of barging people off the ball, and quite frequently barging them when they were nowhere near the ball.

The long, rough meadow grass was something of a hazard, but that was the least of the problems we faced. The Moat Gardens were used by dog owners on a daily basis. Not just for the beasts to exercise, although that may have been their excuse, but as far as we could ascertain, to evacuate their bowels. The dogs that is, not the owners. But hey! I can't even be certain of that.

What I can be certain of, however, as it is indelibly stamped in my memory, is that our soccer games were played on a pitch liberally dotted with piles of dog shit. The old stuff wasn't too bad, all dried up and harmless. It raised clouds of dust if you trod on it, but the new stuff, the gleaming pyramids of recently dropped Fido waste, was a real hazard. Treading in it was one thing. Falling in it was another thing altogether. Some boys went home quite literally covered in poo from head to foot.

I learnt to sidestep the more obvious piles, but those loads dumped in the longer grass were like hidden land mines. You'd be heading for goal, the ball at your feet, swerving and sprinting, dodging tackles, feinting and lunging and suddenly, kersplosh, you were in it.

It slowed the ball up something chronic and nobody would stand near to the next boy who headed it for hours afterwards.

I have no idea whether the Moat Gardens still exist or whether they have been ponced up and gentrified with flower beds and benches and polite notices to dog owners inviting them to use the "doggie-loos" provided by the council or indeed whether dogs are totally banned.

But the Moat Gardens in their heyday, that length of springy turf with its coating of excrement, was where we learned to play real football, dozens of us, scruffy, rough, noisy boys who, impervious to the whining sound of passing trolley-buses in the Fulham Palace Road and the yelping of countless mutts, all dreamed of becoming the next Stanley Matthews or Tommy Lawton or, in my case, the next Ronnie Rooke.

The Festival Of Fulham

Two years before young Princess Elizabeth was crowned Queen of England, the country celebrated the centenary of the great 1851 Exhibition with a spectacular festival on the South Bank of the Thames.

My father reminded me that my grandfather, Quartermaster-Sergeant Harry Frank Turner, had been born a year after the Great Exhibition and was therefore, as he put it, "a genuine child of the glorious Victorian age".

Dad had an extraordinary sense of nostalgia for what he referred to as our "finest century since Agincourt". Born in 1898, three years before the Queen's death in 1901, he too claimed to be a child of the Victorian era.

Although I found this hankering for a vanished past somewhat depressing as a sixteen year old, I nevertheless looked forward to visiting the South Bank celebrations in 1951 with enthusiasm.

Eric, who lived in Ringmer Avenue, said his dad and his uncle had worked in the crew that helped erect the fabulous "Skylon", a 300-foot tower that resembled a giant silver cigar and dominated the skyline of London for miles around. When Eric's dad, a wiry labourer and ex-merchant seaman, suggested we make up a party and visit the South Bank, I was delighted.

My school, sloane, was planning a visit for us, but the chance of going privately, as it were, with a man who had helped put up the Skylon, was too good to pass over.

By the time we had gathered a half dozen or so Fulham lads to make up a group, we had elevated Eric's dad to a position of high magnificence. Indeed, in my school diary that year, I made a note that I was "going to visit the Skylon which Eric Hastings's dad erected". It rapidly became established that the ubiquitous Mr. Hastings, five feet six inches tall, generously tattooed and of a wrinkled, but benign countenance, had not only put up the Skylon single-handed, but had somehow been involved in its design too.

It was clear to us all that Fulham had every right to be proud of its brilliant, creative resident who lived in Ringmer Avenue and rode a bike with the insouciance naturally associated with a latter day Brunel.

The much anticipated day for the visit arrived and, clutching a packed lunch in a greaseproof bag, I joined my Fulham stalwarts, and led by the engineering colossus himself, we boarded a bus and headed "up West".

On what had once been 25 acres of rough land still scarred from German bombing and on the very banks of the Thames, stood a concrete edifice of dramatic design, the Festival Hall, and a rotund structure known as the Dome of Discovery. There were cafes and pavilions and coffee stalls and men selling balloons and crowds of Londoners jostling and gawping at the great, soaring, phallic Skylon. The Skylon that Brian's dad had built!

Awesome or what!

We toured the pavilions, we gazed at the 12-ton steam locomotive inside one of them, we giggled at Henry Moore's sculpture and ate ice cream and chocolate and buttered buns and then consumed our own sandwiches that our mothers had dutifully prepared that morning.

We looked at the big Guinness clock and we rode on the Watersplash and we mingled with the crowds and we were infected by a sense of great excitement. The 1940s had been grey and pinched. War-weary Londoners had put their love of carnival and fun into hibernation, but now, in 1951, this surely was the dawn of a spectacular new age and we, the sixteen year olds, were going to be the inheritors of this wonderful era.

We came home on the bus in late afternoon, exhausted but happy. We'd sat on spiky modern chairs in a garishly decorated cafe and made critical comparisons with our parents' lumpy Uncut Moquette three piece suites. We'd seen girls on the Watersplash showing their legs as the wind caught their cotton frocks and blew them up over their waists. We'd seen people eating spaghetti — in the open air. Decadence, sex, danger, a veritable cocktail of forbidden fruits and we'd been there. We'd been a part of it.

When we arrived home, I told my parents about our day at the Festival and my father nodded sagely. "Sounds O.K." he said, but added darkly, "I doubt if it was as good as the Great Exhibition."

Mother, however, who later visited the Festival with friend, thought it was wonderful.

Later that year, the Conservatives were returned to government and for reasons that seemed incomprehensible at the time, even to my father, ordered the dismantling of the whole show, including Eric's dad's Skylon.

Mum whispered a blasphemy when it happened, "I wish I'd voted Labour now," she said.

Dad looked as if he'd been poked in the eye with a sharp stick.

Later she recanted, to Dad's great relief, but we all still remained baffled by the Tories' act of vandalism.

In my school diary later that year, I referred to the Great South Bank Show as "the Festival of Fulham". Why, I can only guess.

It was either an unconscious Freudian slip or, more likely, a deliberate tribute to Eric's dad from Ringmer Avenue who built the whole damn thing, spiky modern furniture and the mighty Skylon included.

The Man In Black

I sat next to the big brown radio as the valves began to glow behind the wire mesh. It crackled and whined like a wounded animal and, after some knob twiddling, a man's voice, rich and fruity, filled the room. "And now," he intoned, "your appointment with fear. The Man in Black, Mr. Valentine Dyall."

I shivered even though I was wearing my orange and black striped pyjamas and a woollen dressing gown. *Appointment with Fear* was always scary and I loved it.

Mum had lit the fire in the small grate in the back room, but a wooden clothes horse full of damp shirts and towels had been placed in front of it to dry, so very little heat flowed into the room. Dad was in his chair by the fire, still wearing his policeman's serge trousers, but he had put on a pair of check slippers with rubber soles. He was smoking a Player's Navy Cut and inhaling deeply.

I was fascinated by the way he could hold smoke down inside his lungs for what seemed like minutes. Then, usually when he was talking, the smoke would come out of his mouth and nose in thin grey puffs. When he drew on the cigarette, the tip glowed bright red and the ash lengthened. His trick was to see how long the ash grew before it fell off under its own weight.

238

He kept all his cigarette stubs in a tin and when he ran out of those in the packet, he would roll his own from these dog ends. This involved peeling off the thin paper and shredding the tobacco loose so that it could be rolled between the Rizla papers. Those dog ends must have been so saturated with nicotine that each puff must have been as potent as a whole new cigarette.

After "the Man in Black", I went to bed in the bedroom I shared with my sister, Mary. She was on tour with Ivor Novello's Dancing Years in Leeds, where Dad had contacted a local police sergeant to "keep and eye out for Mary".

Going on tour, for a girl still in her teens, was something of a concern to my parents. Mum, however, displayed a stubborn logic over the whole thing. While she worried about her daughter's being in Leeds or Bradford or Wolverhampton, she reminded my dad that he was the one who had declared that all male actors were "poofs" so she'd be safe at least from sexual predators.

My father laughed at this naivety. "That's as maybe," he said, breathing twin plumes of smoke from his nostrils, "but she's up North."

Well, that settled it. "Up North" meant she was in constant exposure to mysterious horrors that even the Man in Black, Mr. Valentine Dyall, couldn't begin to articulate.

Alone in my bedroom, I slid inside the tightly tucked sheets like a letter in an envelope and my bare feet encountered the searing heat of the stone hot water bottle placed there earlier by my mother. Although I tried to recreate the images conjured up by "the Man in Black", my mind kept drifting into a strange Kafka-esque reverie about the north of England. "Up North" sounded exceedingly dodgy to me. And my sister was up there, surrounded by poofs in tights and other nameless terrors.

On this depressing note, I fell asleep, although the last sound I heard outside the bedroom door was the rasp of a Swan Vesta match being struck as Dad lit another cigarette.

A Policeman's Lot

With Father being a policeman, albeit stationed in faraway Rochester Row, I learnt to observe the behaviour and performance of our local Fulham constabulary from a very young age.

Reflecting on this more than half a century later, I realise that the "legend" of the old bobby on the beat, as depicted in Dixon of Dock Green on television, was neither a legend nor a myth. It was a simple truth. They did "plod" about the street oozing both authority and avuncular charm. They were respected by the local citizens, the law-abiding ones at least, and they did often dispense summary justice on the spot when the right opportunity presented itself.

It would send shivers down the spine of libertarians today and trigger outraged editorials in the *Guardian* and "in-depth" investigations by the BBC into police brutality, corruption, mendacity, criminality, sexism, ageism, racism, narcissism and probably fascism as well. Why? Because the dispensation of summary justice often involved clipping recalcitrant young yobboes around the ear or placing the not inconsiderable Metropolitan Police boot up the rear of more mature offenders even as they were actually in the execution of their crime.

One balmy June day in 1948, a local burglar was caught with one leg over a garden wall in Kilmaine Road. He had just relieved the householder of some valuables, petty cash, cheap jewellery and, perhaps significantly, a meat pie.

In 2002, any policeman unfortunate enough to catch a miscreant in such a delicate situation, would be required to follow a complex and ludicrous routine culminating in a blizzard of form-filling back at the station, if indeed he actually made an arrest. If he seized the fellow's arm in a mildly aggressive fashion, he would thereafter dread the receipt of a summons from some sharp human rights lawyer claiming he had used "disproportionate" force in making the arrest. If a prosecution followed, the chances of a conviction would be about 50–50, and the punishment? A safari holiday? Counselling by a vegetarian member of Amnesty International with sandals and a beard?

In 1948, things were a bit different. The lad caught with his leg half over the wall in Kilmaine Road with his booty in a paper bag, wasn't arrested. He was given a sharp smack around the head with the policeman's leather glove, made to return the stolen goods to the house whence they came and told, with the policeman's face inches away from his own, that "if he was caught nicking anything again, anything, any time, he'd not only get another clip round the ear, but be marched, frog-marched even, round to his Mum's house and exposed to his family as the petty little thief he was."

How do I know this? Simple. The burglar was a mate of mine who lived in Ringmer Avenue. He told me all about it in technicolour detail. I don't know whether he re-offended or not because we lost touch when his family moved to Putney, but what I do know is that the way the local bobby dealt with him, left him far from resentful, but feeling an almost reluctant respect for the local copper on the beat.

My father was full of hair-raising tales about the policeman's lot in 1940s London, but he always took care to emphasise that things were even tougher in the 1920s and 1930s.

Even as a child of eleven, I knew there was an element of exaggeration and embroidery in Father's tales, but he was a remarkably good storyteller.

Walking alone in the foggy streets of London down some of Pimlico's most notorious thoroughfares, armed only with a whistle and a truncheon, my father faced down countless threats from opium-crazed Chinese sailors (though just what they were doing in Pimlico was never quite clear), attacks by burly drunks at pub closing time (much more credible), hysterical assaults by prostitutes who, their clothing disarranged, would fling themselves at Father, either begging protection from some cut-throat pimp or occasionally offering fleshy services entirely free of charge. Sternly, Father told us as we sat there, mouths agape, "I, of course, refused."

Later I would ask my mother what exactly these fleshy services were. She would tut-tut and blush and slip a sly look at Father and tell me to drink up my Bovril.

But the adventures Dad had! James Bond didn't even come into it. Or even Sexton Blake.

There were apparently certain streets in central parts of London down which no policeman would venture alone. I can't remember all the names, except one — Cable Street, in Stepney. Now clearly, this was a hotbed of nameless terrors. Every mean terraced house contained a murderer, an axe maniac, an armed assassin from Central Europe (always Central Europe, I wonder why?), or a deranged woman who, like all the others, would explode onto the street displaying more naked skin than was considered appropriate even in Cable Street.

But even for allowing for Dad's love of hyperbole, he was a veritable treasury of folk tales about police work in London during the first half of the 20th century.

In the 1940s, the local bobbies patrolled the streets on foot although, just occasionally, you would observe one of the older ones, pink-cheeked and as plump as an apple, gliding along the Fulham Palace Road on a bicycle.

My father cycled to work wearing a mackintosh over his uniform with his helmet in a saddlebag. The only thing that gave his status away were the boots. Size 10 1/2, thick soled and studded with Blakeys and polished to a sheen that would have brought a smile to the lips of a Sandhurst sergeant-major.

When he retired after 25 years in the force, I asked if he would give me his helmet. "Absolutely not," he said, "that helmet is government property." He kept his boots though. They never wore out.

244

The Tea Lady's Window

In 1941, my mother pinned a sheet of paper to the door of her tiny kitchen. On it, in her own spidery hand, was a list of foodstuff that served as one person's ration for a week.

Bacon and ham	4oz
Sugar	8oz
Butter	2oz
Tea	2oz
Cheese	1oz
Jam	2oz
Meat (by price)	1 shilling

We were a family of four and in spite of rationing, I was never conscious of being short of food. Indeed, my mother's proud boast was that she always had food in the house and could, and indeed did, rustle up a substantial snack at a moment's notice.

Callers, whatever their mission, were always offered food. If I took a friend home from school, even if it was mid-afternoon, mum would produce food. Sandwiches hastily sliced and buttered, the ubiquitous cup-cake or hunk of cold rice pudding.

Considering we had no refrigerator or much cold storage, this was something of an achievement. The cellar, however, was cool enough to keep milk fresh for a couple of days or so.

The ability to feed people at any time of the day or night was, I believe, the inevitable result of having a policeman as head of the family. Dad's hours were, in a word, erratic. Night duty, early turn, ceremonial overtime and so forth, often meant Mother's cooking a fried breakfast for dad at four o'clock in the afternoon after his brief sleep following night duty.

In the next street to ours, Dorncliffe, lived a single lady in a tiny ground-floor flat. Her only companion, as far as we could make out, was a large, flea-bitten red setter with a limp. This lady, in her 50s at least, doted on this mangy pooch and, we suspected, gave him her meat ration each week. She was tall and as thin as a rail and wore a long, patched overcoat and a tight-fitting hat with a long feather.

Mother, whose instinct for helping the needy and the lonely was legendary, soon established that this woman was a dedicated tea-drinker and her pitiful ration of 2oz a week was scarcely enough to slake her craving for the amber fluid. Mother then determined that thenceforth, we would give this woman another 2oz from our own family ration of 8oz.

A ritual was quickly established whereby I would be dispatched to Dorncliffe Road once a week and place a packet of tea on a ledge inside a small window by the front door of this woman's flat. The window, by pre-arrangement, was always left open.

This task I performed throughout the war years and beyond and let me confess that to this day I still don't know what that woman's name was. "Go," Mother would say, "and put this in the tea lady's window." That is how she was referred to. She was the tea lady.

There were others too who benefited from my mother's largesse. Our immediate next door neighbour, Mrs. Gear, a frail, elderly stroke victim, married to the patrician Mr. Gear, hairdresser to Whites Club in Piccadilly, was apparently entirely sustained by custard as she had difficulty in swallowing solids. Custard powder, in greaseproof packets, was therefore thrust through Mrs. Gear's letter box on a regular basis.

I once had to write an essay at my primary school, Sherbrooke Road, and caused a frisson of concern when under the heading "What I did last week," I wrote, truthfully, "On Tuesday I put a packet of Mazawatti in the tea lady's window and on Thursday I put some custard through Mrs. Gear's letter box."

The benign and avuncular Mr. Downey, our form master, peered at me over his half-moon glasses and asked gently if that was indeed what I did last week.

"Oh yes," I replied. "I do it every week." I think he marked me down as an eight year old with an overheated imagination.

There was in Fulham, in the 1940s, a thriving black market and if you knew the right people and were prepared to pay cash, any number of exotic items could be obtained. Naturally my father frowned on this practice and we were all forbidden to accept or buy anything that was still rationed from these "spivs", as they were called. I was always suspicious that little Des across the road was getting his hands on more milk chocolate than seemed absolutely necessary, but then I could be wrong. It could have been somebody copying my mother and stuffing a bar or two of Cadbury's Dairy Milk through his letter box each week.

Imagination

My father was a consummate storyteller. Not only did he treat my sister and to his famous condensed versions of the classics, *King Solomon's Mines* in three fifteen-minute episodes for example, or *Pickwick Papers*, in six ten-minute episodes, he was also a man of great imagination and while never ambitious, remaining a police sergeant for most of his career in the Met, he was a prodigious reader and observer of the human condition.

As a policeman, he saw life in all its rawness and frailty and was ceaselessly fascinated by the sheer variety of people with whom he made contact. He was a "watcher". He could sit for hours when off duty on a park bench and watch the passing throng.

But it wasn't just idle curiosity that prompted this sedentary occupation. He used to like inventing lives and backgrounds for the strangers who wandered by.

I'd sit with him and listen to him construct these wonderful fantasy histories about people he'd never met. A stout man with a limp would pass in front of us and that would be enough to trigger off his imagination. "Poor chap. Kept locked up in a small attic room by his wicked stepmother until he was twelve, hence the waxy complexion and flabby body. A sad case. Almost certainly a gas board employee. You know why he limps? I'll tell you. After being locked up by his stepmother for years, he finally snapped and kicked the door down. Broke his foot. Then he murdered her. Never been convicted. My colleagues are still on the case."

It was all the most ridiculous nonsense and I loved it. You could sit there and make up these fabulous lives and pass an hour or two just letting your imagination run riot. I must confess, I still do it, usually on trains or aeroplanes.

On those rare occasions just after the war when my parents took us on holiday to Swanage, we would stay in a small boarding house close to the seaside. Within hours, all of the other guests would have had past lives and histories constructed by my father.

When I was very young, I actually believed the stories, marvelling at how my father could know so much about all these people. Just imagine, we're sitting in the small dining room of a terraced guest house enjoying fried eggs and chips for breakfast and we are surrounded by: an Austrian baron who eats Alsatians back in Vienna, a middle aged widow who is the world's knitting champion, a child with a pointy head who was once thrown like a dart by his parents at a cork darts board when he was six, a sad married couple who have recently robbed a mail train of many thousands of pounds, but are too nervous to spend their booty too ostentatiously and thus book themselves into the modest hostelry to avoid detection. The fatal clue? The deciding clincher that tells my father of their staggering wealth? They order a second helping of egg and chips at breakfast and do not wince even slightly when the landlady, herself an axemurderess and transvestite ex-nun, tells them in frosty tones, arms folded over her flowered apron, that the second helping "costs extra".

Happy days.

At age thirteen and with my hormones flaring and spluttering like Catherine wheels, I was constantly imagining other people's sex lives. Having had zero sexual experience myself, the "internal lives" I created for my unsuspecting victims were invariably exotic, but at the same time fatuously naive. Across the road from us lived a woman, tallish and dark haired. She lived alone with her young son of ten as her husband was either dead or gone, or probably both. I heard my mother once remark that this woman was "proud of her swan-like neck". I only caught this tiny fragment of conversation, but it was enough to open the floodgates of my imagination.

A woman without a husband, living across, the road, who was "proud of her swan-like neck". Ye Gods, what fertile ground. Naked except for a glittering diamond necklace around her 40-year-old, but admittedly swan-like, neck, she would clearly be seeking sexual solace with various tradesmen who called at her house.

I saw them coupling, her swan-like neck swaying above the shoulder of the milkman, Owen, as he pinned her to the bed. He, of course, remained fully dressed even down to his steel-tipped boots.

Then there was the tiny, almost dwarf-like man who collected insurance premiums in his tweed suit and

251

bicycle clips. He was driven in a frenzy of lust to licking her swan-like neck while she clenched him between prodigiously meaty thighs.

Poor woman. If she only knew that I was onto her little game.

She might come tottering out of the house on high heels and wearing a blue cloth coat with a fake fur collar and a slash of vermilion lipstick to drag a recalcitrant ten-year-old son to school, but in the theatre of my mind, just ten minutes earlier she had allowed the man with a wart on his nose from the gas board to ravish her on the stairs.

She was always starkly unclothed. The tradesmen always fully dressed. And always the focus of their craving was the swan-like neck. She once did it with an electrician in the front room. He, poor wretch, had tried to bite the swan-like neck. I'd read in Hank Jansen books that men in the grip of mindless passion were given to neck-munching, so it would be unexceptional, even inevitable that an electrician with a bag of spanners, frayed wire and tiny screwdrivers would sink his dentures into that column of white, undulating flesh.

So vivid did my imaginings become that I would look hard at the poor woman's neck when she emerged from her house to see if I could spot bite marks.

The desire to create fantasy sex-lives for other people passed eventually, shortly after I placed my hand on the naked breast of a fourteen-year-old girl at Smudger Smith's flat in Walham Green. It was my first real sexual experience. Not much at all. Just a hot little hand grasping a pale adolescent breast.

But it broke the spell. God knows why. From that moment, I never again saw the woman across the road in my fevered imagination coupling with tradesmen or having her swan-like neck licked and nibbled by horny-handed sons of toil. If I'd been born an American and told the story of my teenage fantasies, I would certainly have been categorised as "disturbed". Even crazy. But I was just a lad in Fulham with bit of an imagination. I blame Dad. I got it from him.

Ennui

A large number of people living in Fulham during the 1940s had never been abroad, not even to the Isle of Wight. My parents had a friend who had not only never been abroad, but boasted that he had never been "up West" to Piccadilly. He avoided it because he disliked bus travel and there was no way he was going to cycle there just to be robbed or even murdered by the swarms of cut-throats, footpads and maniacs who, he was utterly convinced, lurked on every street corner from Piccadilly to Holborn Viaduct.

His name was Arnold, but to my sister and I, he was Uncle Arnold. His wife Beryl, not unnaturally, was called Aunty Beryl.

Arnold was a small, rotund man with bulging eyes and tiny feet. He was an employee of the gas board at Walham Green, where he had toiled as a clerk for 25 years. Indeed, he had worked there since leaving Munster Road School when he was fifteen. Unfit for military service, he had therefore avoided being sent abroad during the war and remained steadfastly at the gas board among the buff folders, invoices, filing cabinets and rubber bands performing whatever arcane tasks were allotted to him.

He would occasionally engage me in conversation and offer a range of advice about my future life and prospects because, he once explained, he'd "kept an eye on me" and was "a good friend of my father". In fact, he wasn't a good friend of my father. He was tolerated by my father only because Mother was a proper friend of Aunty Beryl.

Uncle Arnold was a boring man. He was so utterly and completely, buttock-clenchingly boring that the yawns he induced were so huge that they threatened to crack your jawbone.

"I could get you a job at the gas board," Arnold said once. "I have influence there."

When I indicated as politely as possible that such a career prospect was not filling my young heart with eager anticipation, he proceeded to regale me with the benefits of working long-term, for the gas board at Wallham Green.

"Look at me," he would say, patting his waistcoat in a complacent gesture, "25 years, man and boy. Never missed a day off work. I can walk to the board in ten minutes. Back home to Clonmel Road for lunch. Finish at five-thirty. Home again by quarter to six. Regular wages. Every Friday. No mucky work involved. Never touched a gas pipe in my life. Never owned a pair of overalls. Senior clerk. Well respected. Trusted. A steady job. What more can you ask?"

As the horror of this grisly job definition sank home, I tried to deflect the conversation to lighter matters. "Do you like football?" was my idiotic question. God knows why I asked.

"Certainly not," said Arnold sternly. "Crowds. You can get crushed in a crowd. I like bowls though. A nice game of bowls. Aunty Beryl and I play bowls. We never go away for our holidays. To the seaside or anything like that. We stay home and go to the bowling green at Bishop's Park. The gas board have outings, to Hastings and places like that. We never go. I'm excused. Travel sickness."

"I might become a policeman like Dad," I lied, hoping to bring this stultifying conversation to an end.

Arnold's eyes bulged even further from their sockets. "Now don't get me wrong," he protested, "your dad does a fine job. But that's not for you. You're a more refined sort of person. You're at the grammar school. No. You'd be very happy at the gas board. When you're sixteen, I'll put a word in for you."

My sense of limp nausea increased at this grotesque prospect. "No, honestly, Uncle Arnold. Anyway I've got to do my National Service when I'm eighteen."

Now it was Arnold's turn to look mortified. "Oh yes. Of course. Get a home posting. Don't volunteer for anything. Oh dear. Alright then, when you come out of the RAF, I'll speak to the gas board then."

I explained gently that I wasn't going into the RAF if I could help it. Dad had been in the Royal Engineers and Grandad, a career soldier in the King's Royal Rifle Corps. "He served 20 years in India," I said.

At this point Arnold gave me up. I think his plan to adopt me as a protégé and future stalwart at the gas board at Walham Green foundered at this moment.

Arnold lived to a ripe old age and died, I am told, a happy and contented man. I don't think he went to Heaven, and certainly not to Hell; both were too far away. He's probably in limbo, his spirit lurking in the narrow streets around Walham Green, hovering outside the building that once housed the gas board, patting his waistcoat and gazing into the middle distance with his watery, bulging eyes.

My father, whose imagination sometimes bordered on the fantastic, had a theory about the cause of Uncle Arnold's protruding eyes.

During a domestic dispute with his wife, Aunty Beryl, she had thrown a handful of cake crumbs in his face. In his attempt to wipe the fragments of fruit, flour and sugar from his eyes, he had inadvertently pushed some of them into the corner of his eyeballs, blinked a few times and bing! They had lodged themselves behind his eyes.

Overcome with remorse, Aunty Beryl, with the aid of a teaspoon, then scooped Arnold's eyeballs out of their sockets and as they lay hanging on his cheeks, still connected by a thread of tissue, flushed out the rogue cake crumbs with warm water.

The brilliant operation, performed by a woman in a pinny and headscarf, arms still dusted with flour, was then completed by pushing Arnold's eyeballs back into their sockets with the teaspoon handle.

To her lifelong chagrin, and Arnold's too, she couldn't get them all the way back to their original position, so poor, boring Arnold spent the rest of his life with sticky-out eyes.

Shortly before my father died in 1967, I casually mentioned the cake-crumbs-eyeball-teaspoon legend to him and asked if there was a shred of truth in it.

Dad's reply was cryptic. "Oh yes. A shred certainly. Not much of a shred, but a shred all the same. And the cake was of the crushed almond variety."

High Fashion 1947 Style

In 1947, when I was twelve, my sister Mary had already started her stage career in the chorus of Ivor Novello's the Dancing Years. This was followed by a small singing part in C.B. Cochran's *Bless the Bride*. It was something of a thrill even to a boy with a tin ear like myself to realise that my own sister was in a West End show.

Mum used to travel up to the strand via Piccadilly to meet my sister after the performance at the Adelphi Theatre and occasionally, very occasionally, I would tag along and wait backstage with Mum for Mary to come scampering off in full costume, make-up and wig.

My first sniff of greasepaint however, didn't generate the aching desire in my little soul to become an actor myself. I thought it was a career that was perfectly acceptable for a girl, but for a fellow? Dad's awful warning that all male theatricals were likely to be predatory "poofs" rang ominously in my ears.

Much later, after National Service, I did toy with the idea of going to drama school, but instead became a salesman, which I suppose amounts to the same thing in the end.

It was felt that as a professional artist, Mary should dress in the up-to-the-minute clothes and, minuscule though her wages were, she was one of the first Fulham girls to sport the "New Look".

In April 1947, Christian Dior had unveiled his magnificent Corolle dine. Full skirts were now all the rage. They hung down to mid-calf and afforded a tantalisingly brief glimpse of petticoat. Shoulders were padded and the whole "look" was unashamedly romantic - a welcome antidote to the drab, colourless wartime years.

But the New Look wasn't welcomed by everyone. Harold Wilson, then a very junior minister in the Attlee Labour government, claimed it was an irresponsible waste of cloth and the austere Chancellor of the Exchequer, Stafford Cripps, a Dickensian figure of forbidding appearance, even tried to persuade the British Guild of Designers to stick with shorter skirts.

Some womens' libbers of the 1940s suspected the New Look was some kind of male trick to force women back into, A "fragile, cagedbird" style of dress.

But my sister and others ignored these dire, whingeing pecksniffs and soon the rustle of taffeta could be heard on every high street in the land.

For men however, fashion was just a word. The Teddy Boy look was still a few years away and to twelve year olds like myself and most teenage boys, clothes were things you wore to keep warm. Most of us managed, even in school uniform, to contrive to look as if we had just emerged from a major bomb explosion or shipwreck.

One memorable day in 1947, our whole family went for a walk in Bishop's Park and by the great fields that ran alongside the River Thames. Dad looked every inch the off duty copper in his long black overcoat, Homburg hat and yellow knitted gloves.

Mum's tiny figure was clad in a mauve topcoat and a little hat, like a cake, with a long feather sticking out of the top.

Mary, the singer, who would shortly accelerate her career and join the chorus of Sadler's Wells Opera, was in the New Look. All swirling skirts and high heeled shoes and an even sillier hat than Mum, but they looked, I suppose, extraordinarily chic, especially for Fulham.

I remember what I was wearing only because of what happened that afternoon. It was grey trousers, a grey pullover and sandals. They were perfectly reasonable clothes, but the verdict that was passed on my appearance that day was that I looked like a "hooliganish Just William." A hooliganish Just William!

O.K. So my hair was like a lavatory brush and my pipestem white legs were clad in wrinkled black socks and my sandals were a bit scuffed.

But a hooliganish Just William?

It was my sister who coined the phrase. Worse was to follow.

As we entered the bandstand area of the park, my later trysting ground and boulevard of broken dreams, Mary declared that I was not to walk next to them. I had to fall in several paces behind for fear that somebody might assume I was "with them."

Disowned by my own family! As other strollers passed by, Dad would raise his Homburg in greeting, while Mary and Mum, peacock proud, would enjoy the admiring glances of the young swains from Putney who had crossed the bridge and were partaking of the cleansing atmosphere and leafy greenery of Bishop's Park.

It was later that day that I heard my mother utter the immortals judgment that I was not only a "hooliganish Just William", but that I looked as if I had been "dragged through a hedge backwards".

This last phrase has resonated down the years and I found myself uttering it twenty years later when I was being fitted for my first Saville Row Suit.

"I want the waist to be narrow," I told the tailor at Huntsmans, "I don't want to look as if I've been dragged through a hedge backwards."

The tailor's expression was one of monumental grief. "But of course not, Sir," he gasped. "In Saville Row we don't make suits, we build them, Sir."

I'm sure he thought I was casting doubts on the crisp efficiency of his cutters, but all I was doing was unconsciously hoping that the ghost of my father and my ageing mother would not think that my huge extravagance on a Saville Row three-piece suit, complete with cloth covered cuff buttons and a waistcoat with lapels would, when worn by their son, make him look like a man who had been dragged through a hedge backwards. Or indeed, God forbid, like a "hooliganish Just William".

There was a second-hand clothes shop in the Fulham Road which my mother used as a last resort when kitting me out in those first, febrile, fashion-conscious years after the war. My first overcoat came from this shop: a thing like a blanket with sleeves and no waist. Mum paid £2 two shillings for it and I loathed it. It smelled of mothballs and, I swear, rancid sweat. It had big bone buttons and a shiny lining with a curious criss-cross pattern. The pockets were ten-gallon jobs full of fluff and nameless greasy little objects that stuck to the insides.

It was also too big for my skinny twelve-year-old frame. If I buttoned it up to the throat and then turned swiftly to the right or left, the bloody coat remained facing to the front. When Mum purchased it, the man in the shop, a wizened fellow with a pronounced hump, made me try it on in front of a full length mirror. I'm absolutely sure he stood behind me and pinched the cloth at the back together to give the impression that it actually fitted me.

"He'll grow into it," Mum explained later when Dad commented that the coat looked vaguely like a tent. Much as I tried to avoid wearing it, fearful of the screaming hysteria it would provoke among my friends, the occasional cold snap meant it couldn't always be avoided. "I know where you got that bleeding coat," Doug Wilson once commented. Doug was my friend who would later become my training partner at St. George's Bodybuilding Club when we both took up bodybuilding. "Yes", sneered Doug. "I know where you got it."

"Where?" I asked defensively.

"Quasimodo's," he said, pronouncing it with a thick French accent.

My knowledge of French literature at that time being at its nadir, I merely nodded. "Yes," I said, "down the Fulham Road."

Well it sounded good, "Quasimodo's, Outfitters to the Gentry."

How did I know the damn coat made me look like a hunchback?

At Last 1948

Nineteen forty-eight was an interesting year. The Fulham Borough Council was described in the *Daily Telegraph* as being one of the most forward looking in the whole of London. For some mysterious reason, this pleased my mother but infuriated my father. "How can they be forward looking?" he would suddenly snap over his mashed potato and pork sausage (at least 50% bread), "How can they?"

Mum would wipe her hands on her pinny in a defiant gesture. "Well, look at Bishop's Park. It's lovely. All that planting. And they've painted the bandstand."

Dad would fork down an enormous dollop of potato and then, after brief consideration, fire off his devastating rejoinder. "The street lights in Burnfoot Avenue are a disgrace!"

Now as there was no immediate way for my mother to check the validity of this statement, it was allowed to stand. Half-time score: Father 1, Mother and Fulham Council 0.

I cycled down Burnfoot Avenue two days later and checked out the situation for myself. In broad daylight. It was therefore impossible to assess the quality of illumination provided by these cast iron sentinels of municipal public spiritedness.

A week or so later, I re-visited Burnfoot Avenue at dusk and, lo and behold, three of the lamps were out of operation in that long avenue.

I returned to Hestercome and relayed the tragic news to my mother. She took it on the chin and shrugged. "Oh alright," she said, but added darkly, "but it has to be weighed up against the marigolds in Bishop's Park. It's a blaze of colour this time of year."

For some reason, this reply confused me. I found it hard to draw an intellectual comparison between bright orange flowers in our park and faulty iron lampposts in Burnfoot Avenue.

A week later, the three defunct lamps were alight again and my mother conveyed this supreme intelligence to Dad as soon as he'd propped his bike in the hall and removed his cycle clips. Father 1, Mother and Fulham Council 1.

The matter was never discussed again.

Nineteen forty-eight was also a year when, at Sloane School, our headmaster, Guy Boas, arranged a visit to the cinema for members of the school Shakespeare Society. Twenty or so of us were to see Laurence Olivier in *Hamlet*, a treat that most of us looked forward to with mixed emotions. We liked acting in the school plays well enough, but our apprehension was triggered by the fact that we'd have to miss football on the afternoon of the visit. The school curriculum couldn't cope with both soccer and the bard on the same day.

Curiously, I didn't find Olivier's Hamlet entirely to my taste. I think the blonde wig, or hair dye, put me off, making him look like an escapee from the Royal

Ballet School, especially in those buttock-clinging tights.

But Shakespeare, being a celebration of the richness of the English language, remained of interest and pleasure to me, not just for the rest of 1948, but forever. More than 30 years later, at the Old Vic, I saw Olivier play Othello with Frank Finlay as Iago and Maggie Smith as Desdemona. In fact I saw it six times including two matinées: the greatest performance I believe I shall ever see.

English words and their pronunciation and their meaning played a continuing role in my life during 1948. At Sloane Grammar, history was taught to us by the magnificently eccentric Mr. Berkeley. A thin, aesthetic master whose enthusiasm for his subject was legendary. He would act out various roles during his exhortations about, for example, the Battle of Bosworth Field, crying aloud in pain as an arrow pierced his chest or rallying the troops with wild gestures, chalk in hand, gown flying like Dracula's cloak as he lived each part to the full.

Mr. Berkeley was what we Fulham lads called a bit of a toff. He spoke with a cultivated, public school accent that was only a degree or so less aristocratic than the headmaster's. Both men, for example, said "hice" instead of "house", or in our case "owse". Mr. Berkeley also spoke slowly, enunciating each word like a morsel of tasty food. "Open — your — Happolds," he was wont to exclaim. Happold was the publisher of one of our school history books. "Open — your — Happolds," therefore, was a call to arms, a rallying cry and a goad.

267

Opening the slightly dog-eared Happold on my desk, I knew we were in for a treat of histrionics by Mr. Berkeley once he got warmed up. "Imagine the scene on page 37," he would cry in his high-pitched voice, and we would all scramble to find the right page. I can, to this day, still hear the rustle of 38 boys flipping over the pages of their Happolds as Mr. Berkeley gathered up his gown and began pacing the room. "I — am — John-of-Gaunt," he might yell at us, or on another day and another page, "I — speak — to — you — today — on — the — great — field — of — Waterloo, — the — muddy — wastes — strewn — with — French — and — English — dead!!"

One day a curious incident occurred, one that I recorded in my school diary. It was 10th May 1948. We were in the middle of a lesson about the Duke of Wellington as prime minister, and his shifting attitude to Catholic emancipation. Mr. Berkeley, to demonstrate Wellington's initial hostility to reform, had suddenly leapt onto a chair and screamed, "No Popery!" which confused me a touch. But it was no matter. What followed was far more significant.

Mr. Berkeley paced between the desks where 38 blazered boys tried to keep an eye on their Happolds and Berkeley as he assumed, rather badly as it happens, an approximation of the Duke of Wellington's patrician drawl.

Suddenly a boy on my left farted. A long, rumbling, trombone-like fart that cut through the classroom like a knife. I laughed. Loudly. Well, it was funny. It is funny. Even to this day the sound of air being expelled with

268

great velocity from another person's bottom is a singularly hilarious thing. Oh alright, it's a bit juvenile. But what the hell.

Mr. Berkeley turned to me and glared. "Turner," he cried, "you — laugh — because — a — boy — makes — an — unfortunate — noise. You — are — a — cheap — Bulgarian!"

This rebuke stunned me. Why a Bulgarian? Were the denizens of this particular part of Central Europe prone to guffaw at wind-breaking? Was it a racial characteristic? Perhaps with religious overtones? Silenced by Mr. Berkeley's reprimand, I returned to my Happold in chastened mood.

It was only when I returned home later that day I realised that what Mr. Berkeley had actually called me was, "a cheap vulgarian".

I think on reflection I'd rather be known as a Bulgarian, cheap or expensive as the case may be; it sounds rather exotic, reminiscent of intrigue on the Orient Express and long, onyx cigarette holders, whereas, quite frankly, vulgarian sounds, well, kind of vulgar.

The only other things of significance I recorded in my diary for 1948 were the official start of the National Health Service, the assassination of Mahatma Ghandi and the publication of a book called, *The Naked and the Dead* by Norman Mailer, which we were warned not to read.

However, there were reports of an utter lack of flatulence throughout the Balkans.

Dead Sexy

Shortly after my twelfth birthday, I saw a man and a woman copulating in the small graveyard that adjoins Fulham's All Saints' Church. It wasn't a particularly spectacular event; both participants were fully dressed, although as the local newspaper would have pruriently described it, their clothing was disarranged.

The act took place behind an ancient gravestone and on a carefully placed raffia mat. The man, on top naturally, wore a long overcoat which concealed most of his body, but his trousers were in a wrinkled concertina around his ankles revealing bone-white calves and shoes which were in serious need of repair.

The woman, for she was a woman rather than a girl, had stockinged, shoeless feet waving either side of his pumping body and her face, red with either passion or effort, rested on his shoulder, her eyes open and unblinking.

Even at twelve, I felt a twinge of guilt at being witness to this private act of passion here among the silent dead and the mildewed stone crucifixes.

After a couple of minutes, I moved away, intrigued but curiously unaroused by what I had seen. My companion, an older boy of fourteen called Jim, wanted to stay longer, but when he saw me walking towards the gravel path away from the spectacle of suburban bacchanalia, he followed, hissing disapproval. "Should a stayed," he whispered. "When 'e gets off, we'll see her tits."

This I doubted, for she was clearly the proud wearer of both a woolly cardigan and a blue mackintosh. "They might have seen us," I protested.

Jim shrugged. "So what?" he said producing a half-smoked Woodbine. "Give 'em a thrill to get caught."

This subtle observation sailed right over my head and we trudged around the back of the church towards the exit that led towards Putney Bridge.

Our visit to the graveyard at All Saints' Church had not been pre planned as a voyeurs' outing, but for a much more esoteric purpose. Jim, who was senior to me at Sloane School, had been set a homework task that required him to write an essay about the "the history of Fulham". He had decided that there was no better place to soak up the past then the old graveyard at All Saints' Church. I tagged along because I knew we would be going on to the Black and White milk bar in Putney afterwards, a most fashionable venue for "older" boys, and I was anxious to demonstrate my sophistication and *élan* by accompanying him.

Before stumbling across the graveyard lovers, we had toured the graves and the little tombs and Jim had made notes on a tiny pad from those inscriptions that had not been obscured by lichen or moss or simply old age.

For some reason, possibly idle curiosity but almost certainly lost in the mists of time, I too scribbled a few words with my bitten pencil on the back of a fag packet that I picked up by the side of a halfsunken marble angel. Later those words, transcribed literally from a couple of headstones, were transferred to my diary. I have no idea why I did it. The bodies over which these inscriptions were engraved had been long dead, mouldering under the Fulham turf, bones crumbling to dust. But they had lived and walked and breathed in the borough when it was an ancient village, surrounded by farms and old fishing boats on the Thames, and when Putney Bridge was a wooden structure suitable for horses and cattle and farm carts.

There was the cracked and tilting monument to the Reverend George Rowley who died in the year 1800 aged 53. How many times over the decades had he stood in the pulpit of All Saints' Church preaching of salvation and hellfire? And what would he have made of the congregation in 1947?

Then there was the monolithic stone headpiece marking the grave of one Thomas Twitchin, a name which induced the hilarious comment from my companion, Jim, that, "he ain't twitchin' any more, is he?" Thomas Twitchin died in Fulham on 2nd October 1798 at the tender age of twenty. Such a short life. Poor Thomas Twitchin. Next to the entry in my diary I wrote the words, "bad luck". This was about as profound a comment as I could muster at the age of twelve.

The experience that day of witnessing two people engaged in an act designed to produce life among the

272

granite sentinels that marked death was certainly memorable. But it wasn't traumatic. My American friends nod gravely when I tell them of it and are convinced that it has left some deep pshycological scar on me. It hasn't. I've felt no compunction to fornicate in a graveyard, not even on a raffia mat. It was just another day remembered in the life of a very ordinary, but curious, Fulham boy.

And, oh yes, I almost forgot. I was christened at All Saints' Church in 1935.

Note: At a recent visit to the All Saints' Cemetery in the summer of 2002, I came across a fine monument that had escaped my notice in 1947. It was raised to the memory of Colonel Thomas Heron, Viscount Renelagh, KCB, who was the founder and commander of the 2nd South Middlesex Rifle Volunteer Regiment in 1859. The Middlesex, of course, was the regiment I joined in 1953 to do my National Service.

Ambition

Benjamin Disraeli once wrote, "Personal distinction is the only passport to the society of the great, but certain it is to enter society, a man must either have blood, a million or a genius."

Teenage boys in Fulham in the early 1950s had a much less sophisticated view of their future. Some of us who had been lucky enough to attain grammar school status, however, did entertain dreams of a career or even, daringly, wealth and celebrity.

But not all of us by any means.

Many of my contempories from school and neighbouring streets had resigned themselves to lives of mundane conformity, displaying what Aneurin Bevan, the great Labour icon, once described as "poverty of ambition".

I don't think that the inadequacies of selective education or the secondary modern schools themselves were entirely the cause of this sad state of affairs. They must take some share of the blame, of course, but I believe the root cause was at home, where under-achieving parents simply couldn't contemplate their children moving up the social scale or clambering through the hierarchy of work.

I knew two boys, brothers, who lived in nearby Doneraile Street. Although very bright and articulate, they had failed to obtain places at grammar school and, even after displaying considerable talent at their secondary modern, both said they never wanted anything more than just a job, and preferably one that didn't throw too much responsibility on their shoulders.

Other friends were horrified that I had not taken up a trade. The concept of the vaguely classical education that I had received at Sloane was a cause for head shaking incomprehension. They had taken apprenticeships as electricians, bricklayers, glaziers or carpenters. They would get jobs. Steady, low-paid jobs. Probably for life.

What would I do? Yes, I could rabbit on like an auctioneer and quote from Shakespeare's plays. But what the hell use was that? Rather poncey was the general verdict. Bit of a no-hoper, if you really want to know.

But at sixteen, and even seventeen, I hadn't the faintest notion, not even a glimmer, of what I wanted to do with my life. In fact, I was little better in my forward thinking than my friends, the brothers from Doneraile Street. What the hell was I going to do?

Learn to speak and write well, my headmaster Guy Boas had urged.

O.K. I could do that, modestly well. But I was no budding Socrates or Charles Dickens. I was just a bit lippy. Looming up was the prospect of National Service. Two years in uniform. Most of my friends viewed it with dread. "Waste of time." "Two years of bullshit." And I wasn't going to university either, which might have allowed me time to formulate some sort of coherent plan for my future.

I began to panic. Older friends, returning from their numbingly boring two years in the RAF at some windblown air force base in Middle England, were settling into their trades, or the clever ones were taking accountancy examinations or joining banks or flogging cheap cosmetics from barrows in the North End Road.

The idea of returning from my National Service and doing any of these things filled me with wrenching despair.

One evening in Bishop's Park, I was talking with Peter Pryke, who's father was a senior reporter on the *Fulham Chronicle*, and he told me that I ought to take an evening course in shorthand, like him, and become a trainee reporter. I could do it comfortably before I was called up for my National Service and then, hey presto, when I returned to civilian life, I would have a qualification I could actually use.

But I didn't do it. Peter Pryke did and became a successful journalist on the *Daily Telegraph*.

My parents, particularly my mother, wanted me to "get on" and have a "nice life", but they weren't able to provide a complete focus for these vague aspirations. That had to come from me.

I left Sloane School in 1952 at the age of seventeen and worked in two totally dead-end jobs in the twelve months prior to my call up. The first one was as a junior clerk with the Queensland Government of Australia's office in The Strand; the second was as a post clerk with *The Economist* newspaper in St.

James's. The work was so boring it made my teeth itch and the only thing I really learned was how to yawn with my mouth shut.

But in 1953, in June, when I put on uniform and joined the Army, something happened. Some tiny explosion in my head. A spark of unfocused but still potent ambition was ignited.

I would succeed.

Somehow. At something.

And my real education began that day in Oswestry, North Wales, when I became a soldier.

After basic training, I went up to the great officer cadet school in Chester, Eaton Hall, the ancestral home of the dukes of Westminster. For a Fulham youth who had never in all his eighteen years been away from home for more than a few days, this was a major turning point in my life.

The other cadets, mostly public school boys, spoke openly of their plans after National Service, university, the law, business, academia, careers which they confidently predicted would bring them wealth, status and happiness. My future after two years' Army service was a bleak, empty landscape.

Day one at Eaton Hall was one I shall forever remember. Newly arrived cadets were assembled inside one of the vast gothic rooms of the hall and subjected to a welcoming address by Lieutenant-Colonel Woodruff of the Royal Sussex Regiment. A languid, aristocratic-looking officer who spoke in an exaggerated drawl, Colonel Woodruff gazed down from the platform where he stood, at the sea of pink, eager faces below.

His opening words remained indelibly planted in my mind and they were: — "Welcome to Eaton Hall Officer Cadet School. Now, you come to us as fellows, and our job is to turn you into chaps."

Noel Coward couldn't have put it any more succinctly.

The regiment I was subsequently commissioned into as a second-lieutenant was the Middlesex, originally located in Fulham. They had just returned from active service in Korea, where they were the first British troops ashore to serve under United Nations' command. After enduring rigorous and bloody fighting, they earned seven battle honours, far in excess of any other unit during that war.

I joined them in Austria after nearly five months of intensive and physically tough officer cadet training, infinitely tougher than the original basic training we had received in Oswestry.

It was here, almost certainly, that I developed the first stirring of serious ambition for my future.

I would succeed. I would acquire status. And wealth. As Disraeli had said, "A man must have either blood, a million or a genius." "Cobblers," I thought, "all you need is determination, hard work and absolute confidence."

But what would I do?

I still didn't have a clue.

For the next two years, however, I just concentrated on being a dashing young subaltern in the famous 57th — The Diehards.

It was the best time of my life.

Fading Memories — And Conclusions

Memories of half a century ago are almost invariably tinted with nostalgia. Months and even years concertina together until half a decade seems like no more than a few months.

My old school diary which covers most of the late 1940s is scarcely a definitive record of the times, rather a series of brief scribbles that in today's marketing-speak would be described as bullet points. The odd word written in my bold, childish hand is enough to conjure a tide of memories, most of them happy ones.

Perhaps I have blotted out the bad times, if there were any, but certain solid milestones remain. I was fortunate in living in an era when a secure, loving family base was the norm for most people.

Fulham was itself a microcosm of London as a whole, possibly of the rest of the country too. The bruises of the Second World War were still painful and slow to heal, but there was a sense of optimism too, at least in our family. Things would get better. My parents wished most fervently for my sister and me to "do well" and get on. It was not considered an act of class betrayal for working-class children to wish to drag themselves upwards by their bootstraps and succeed.

Perhaps it still isn't today, but there is a subtle difference. Those who aspired and then achieved did so without a chip on their shoulders. It wasn't considered bad form to shed proletarian habits and speech patterns as you entered the lush foothills of middle-class territory.

I am amazed and a little saddened to observe today enormously successful people who have achieved dizzying heights in their professions still displaying class envy and deliberately over-cultivating their old prejudices and manners. For God's sake, those people have broken through the class barrier like knives through butter and are living proof that the old upper, middle and lower structures of society are no longer rigid. I and most of my contempories never looked upon the three-class system as a block to progress.

It was a challenge. And we faced it, and we won. No talk then of wanting a "classless" society, which is a fantasy anyway like absolute grace. Let the class system, or the natural pecking order of things, remain.

This said, it is also true that not all my friends and contempories shared this view. I have mentioned in earlier chapters Aneurin Bevan's famously anguished cry about the "poverty of ambition among the working class", but many children now can succeed, however humble their beginnings, provided they have the will — the burning, thrusting, unconquerable will. The barriers are illusory or, at worst, of straw.

There really is no such thing as a classless society. What about America? Do me a favour. They have rich, poor and middling too. Always have had. Always will. And Russia? Post-Communist Russia. Classless? Donnez moi une fracture.

Sweden? Leave it out, please.

Australia? Come on, those rugged, sundrenched diggers with corks dangling from their hats, they're all the same class aren't they? The answer is in the plural and they both bounce.

Difference in income, physique or intelligence, which is really what defines class, is a natural, inevitable phenomenon.

The only thing that matters therefore is to ensure that entry and exit from whatever class structure as society has is easy and not artificially blocked.

Do the words "chest" and "getting" and "off" spring to mind?

My attitudes to all the above were sown in the fertile soil of the Borough of Fulham during those strange, sometimes bland, decades of the 1940s and 1950s.

I grew up in Fulham. I played in its streets and in its parks. I cheered the Lillywhites at Fulham Football Club; I watched master salesmen ply their trade in the North End Road market, marvelling at their quick wit and dazzling patter. I lifted weights at the St. George's Bodybuilding Club, Fulham's embassy in Putney. I spent hours in the Fulham Library absorbing books that ranged from mindless pap to the great classics; I fell in love with Veronica Lake, the American film star, in the velvet darkness of the Broadway Garden Cinema.

I outran a mob of toughs known as the Walham Green Boys and discovered I was no mean sprinter. I discovered the most erotic part of a girl is that four-inch gap of warm thigh twixt stocking top and knicker leg. What the hell happened to that?

I loved school, both primary and grammar. Teachers at both were enthusiasts and it rubbed off. I could have done better, but I didn't. Those tiny seeds of knowledge sown in Fulham didn't bloom until later during post-school and army years.

Finally, to paraphrase another chap whose name eludes me but who was certainly what we used to describe in Fulham as "a diamond geezer", I realised that by being born an Englishman in Fulham and in London, I had drawn first prize in the lottery of life.

Also available in ISIS Large Print:

Bothy to Big Ben

Ben Coutts

Ben Coutts has packed much more into his 80-plus years than most mortals. Before the war he worked as a ponyman in Perthshire and rural Sussex. Once he had joined up, his wartime experiences were hilarious and tragic by turns. He fought in Africa, was seriously wounded in Tobruk, torpedoed on his trip home in the Laconia, bombed, and when he had made it to the UK, began a long recovery after a series of painful operations. He went on to become a farm-manager in the Highlands, a sheep farmer, a leading stock breeder, show judge and broadcaster, and even a would-be Westminster politician.

ISBN 0-7531-9304-3 (hb)
ISBN 0-7531-9305-1 (pb)

I Married Joan

Joan Park

Joan Park's affectionate "autobiography" of her life with her husband, Alex

"What kind of a wife do you think Joan would make?" This was the start of the marriage between Joan, a teacher from Liverpool, and Alex Park, eleven years her senior and from Glasgow. Married in 1953, Joan moved to Glasgow and into a very different world from the one she had known, for Alex expected a wife who stayed at home, brought up the children and kept a good house. She, an experienced teacher, wished to continue her career.

Joan Park's account of her marriage, as seen through her husband's eyes, is humorous and encouraging, a wonderful glimpse into the hardships of the immediate post-War years through the changes of the 1960s and 1970s to the present.

ISBN 0-7531-9988-2 (hb)
ISBN 0-7531-9989-0 (pb)

Down the Cobbled Stones

John Lea

A Cheshire farmer born and bred, John Lea was the youngest of a family of four, born on a small tenanted farm in Mid-Cheshire in 1935.

His childhood memories are of the tough times in the 1920s and 1930s as his father fought to keep the farm alive. There are tales of horses, water mills and the"Smithy", the exciting and profitable war years and above all his love of his life and the countryside in which he made his home.

John was struck down by polio at the age of twenty, and left severely disabled as a result. After a slow recovery, he eventually married and set about building the life that he had always dreamt of.

ISBN 0-7531-9300-0 (hb)
ISBN 0-7531-9301-9 (pb)

Home Kids

Evelyn Stemp

With a voice that touches the heart, Evelyn Stemp recalls the harsh reality of her childhood in care

In the early 1940s, Evelyn Stemp and her two sisters were taken into care following the death of their mother. Evelyn, aged four, and her sister Edie were separated from their little sister Jean for reasons that were never explained to them. Thus began their harsh new regime, from a children's home to being fostered by a cruel couple who confined them to the scullery.

Eventually the girls' fortunes change and they complete their childhood in a happy rural home. But when, in her adult life, Evelyn sets out to discover the mystery family she and her sisters were unaware they had, the memories of neglect come flooding back.

ISBN 0-7531-9972-6 (hb)
ISBN 0-7531-9973-4 (pb)